HOLY
ORDER
RESTORED

Eliyahu ben David

Zarach

Author Online!

For news, resources, updates, teaching, and more visit Eliyahu ben David at:

www.Tsiyon.org

This book has been published on the Internet since 1995 in at least four digital editions under various titles. After many requests from readers to do so, we are now pleased to offer this first actual print edition. The content is essentially the same as the earlier editions but with some updating, editing, and formatting appropriate for this publication.

Published by
Zarach
Salt Lake City, Utah

ISBN-10: 0-9679471-1-1
ISBN-13: 978-0-9679471-1-2

Subject heading:
RELIGION/Biblical Studies/General

1.0

DEDICATION AND ACKNOWLEDGEMENTS

This print edition is no less needed than was the original first written back in 1994 and published digitally starting in 1995. It highlights the often-neglected but vital theme of our Father's way of working in this earth through the leadership of his men—a message that few understand in these days when men have largely lost their way. I'm told by readers that this message has power to set you free to be who you are meant to be, whether you are a man or a woman. To release you to freedom is the real purpose of this book.

I continue to dedicate this book to my Father in heaven, Who called me to this work by grace alone, for the sake of His own Great Name. Next, to The Son, my dearest Friend, Who daily empowers me through the Spirit of sonship. Lastly, to the memory of my departed father, a saint and noble man of God unknown to this world but well known to the courts of heaven. He struggled. He believed. He overcame the enemy in Messiah's mighty Name!

As to acknowledgments, my thanks are, above all, to our Heavenly Father and His Beloved Son for the grace that has led me and sustained me in bringing this message to many over the course of the years. After that, my humble thanks are in order to every member of my family for their many sacrifices so that this book could be published and this work could be done. Know that I love you all, both near and far. Thanks also to many helpful supporters, friends and fellow-workers too numerous to list—all of whom have been and are vital to my efforts.

For this print edition I add my special thanks to my beloved, Dawn, for her invaluable dedication, personal encouragement and inspiration. Secondly, I add my thanks to Dawn for her considerable publishing skills which were so vital to the preparation of my manuscript for publication as a book. Thirdly, yes thirdly, I must also add my thanks to Dawn for seeing the manuscript through a myriad of hoops after its preparation to actually get it published and in your hands. Truly, Dawn is a woman of many hats and each of them is worn with excellence!

As a teacher who finds teachings everywhere I must end these acknowledgements with a lesson. I observe that the unity of thought and action that has put this book into your hands is a real life example of the power that is unleashed when the message of this book is actualized. Read the book and you will understand what I mean!

A Psalm Of David (8:3-9)

When I consider Your heavens, the work of Your fingers,

The moon and the stars, which You have ordained;

What is man, that You are mindful of him?

And the son of man, that You care for him?

For You have made him a little lower than the Angels,

And crowned him with glory and honor.

You have given him dominion over the works of Your hands;

You have put all things under his feet:

All sheep and oxen, yes, all the beasts of the field,

The birds of the heavens, and the fish of the sea,

Whatsoever passes through the paths of the seas.

O YHWH, our Lord,

How excellent is Your Name in all the earth!

Table of Contents:

1

A DREAM, A VISION, A CALL

To God's Chosen Men of the Scattered Twelve Tribes of the Israel of God: I am a man called by Messiah. By His grace He has sent me forth with a message for a prepared people; a people who, in faith, are looking for a spiritual home on this earth transcending anything the Christian religious system has to offer. In the secret places within our spirits we yearn for a city not made with hands, yet on this earth, where God Himself might show forth His glory as a light in the midst of the darkness. This unrelenting vision of a glorious Temple of fleshly stones is not just a foolish and unrealistic dream, as some would have us believe. It is the very intention of our Father in heaven and His Self-sacrificing Son. He gave His life to have such a Bride on this earth, without spot or blemish, and He shall have her.

Past The Boundaries

If God is real and all of the universe is within his scope of knowledge and control then it is perfectly reasonable to assume that he can communicate with any of his creatures. Nevertheless, when it happens for the first time, it often comes as a tremendous shock to the recipient of that communication. It is odd that many of us can believe that God would speak to some ancient sage or saint but at the same time cannot believe that God could or would speak to us personally. That is precisely how I believed for the first thirty years of my life. My primary community during that time was the strict religious sect of which I was a part. That religion set almost all the boundaries in my life and defined who I was. As part of that religion I believed that God had spoken to the ancient Bible writers and had even influenced the more modern leaders of my religion. However; it was absolute heresy to think that God would ever communicate with me personally.

Imagine my shock and surprise when on my thirty-first birthday, in 1981, God came smashing through that mental barrier to communicate with me. In that instance God spoke to me through a dream. It was a dream that even now continues to mold the direction of my life and define the very purpose of my existence.

My identity has become wrapped up with and defined by that dream and another similar and related communication. If at this point you're skeptical, that's probably normal. I'll simply tell you what my experience was and what it means to me. You can do with it what you will.

A Dream From God

In my birthday dream I saw the side of a great wall of sand. It was almost vertical and was something akin to what you would see looking up from inside a sand pit, only very much larger. My view of this was from a distance where I could see the surface crisscrossed by a network of metal tracks forming a gigantic structure of rectangles. Within these rectangles were pitiful, naked, a-sexual people. They were slithering in the sand with metal shackles around their necks by which they were chained with short chains to the metal matrix. This arrangement allowed the people to move around anywhere within the boundaries of the track network, and they did so by very expertly slithering in the sand. They slithered on their bellies because the chains were too short to allow them to stand on their feet. As my gaze took in what was happening in this dream I found it repugnant and terrifying. The people in the dream though, had adapted to their strange bondage to such an extent that it was accepted as perfectly normal.

After taking in the bizarre sight just described, my perspective changed. I found myself standing towards the back of a cave that was located above the metal track network. As I looked out toward the mouth of the cave I saw a man standing with his arms folded, smugly overlooking the entire structure. He was obviously very much in control of it all. At his feet, in the mouth of the cave, the metal tracks converged and were held firmly in place by two metal spikes. The man was confident in his total control of it all. As I continued to watch, I was startled by the lightning swift appearance of another man out of the shadows of the cave. In one quick fluid motion this other mysterious figure pulled the spikes out of the ground, releasing their hold on the metal tracks, after which he jammed them into the forehead of the overlord. After that he disappeared into the shadows. All this happened in a heartbeat.

As I continued to watch, the old man turned around and faced toward me, falling on to his knees. As he looked up into my face I observed the two spikes firmly driven into his forehead with little riverlets of blood forming a strange spider-web pattern on his face. There was an irony in the similarity between the pattern of the metal track network and the pattern the blood was forming on his face. I observed that his power was broken. He was emaciated and powerless as he looked up at me—but he was not dead. As I continued to wonder over this strange vision I observed that although the spikes had been removed the prisoners of the network system didn't know it. They could have gotten free of it but they just continued in their bondage as though nothing had happened. It was strangely anti-climactic. These two factors, that the overlord was not dead and that the people did not know that they had been liberated, filled me with an urgent concern that the figure from the shadows would return to finish what he had started—and when he did it would affect me. It would affect everyone.

At this point I became aware of others in the cave including my family. Men in business suits and ties were coming out of a side corridor of the cave. They were taking people away to have the metal shackles put on their necks so that they could be added to the system. As they reached out to take away my family I reacted with both revulsion and determination, putting out my arms to prevent them. I put my arms around my family and anyone else who would come to me and shouted, "NO! NO! You can't take them! NO"!

The final haunting image of this dream occurred as I looked into my wife's eyes and reached out to her—and she hesitated to come to me. As I woke up, heart pounding, sitting up in my bed in a pool of sweat, shouting "NO! NO!" to the men, I was still in the struggle and did not know if my wife and family would go with them or go with me.

This dream was from God. At the time it occurred I did not believe such a thing was possible and yet I knew absolutely when I woke up that I had had a divine visitation. When God wishes to reveal Himself to an individual that individual knows with certainty that he has encountered God. This dream spoke perfectly to my situation then and what is more important reveals the exalted viewpoint of God regarding matters vital to us all. The truth that I so abruptly encountered is this; God has often communicated with men through dreams and He continues to do so in our day. (See Job 33:15-18, Acts 2:17)

The Meaning Revealed

Through this dream God shattered the boundary which prohibited direct communication from Him. He simply ignored that boundary and flooded my mind with this revelation. The effect on me was monumental. I was shaken and stunned to my very core. I know now that the divine revelation was meant to shatter my boundaries and move me in a certain direction - His direction. I had seen things from His higher viewpoint and I would never be 'normal' again. More about that later. Right now I would like to concentrate on what I have come to understand to be the general meaning of that revelation.

We earthbound humans are slaves to the boundaries of our culture. One important reason for this is our short and finite existence. We grow up and are indoctrinated in a certain culture, live within the limited realm of thought and experience common to our own time and place and then die. How little we really know of the big picture! Consider for a moment the higher viewpoint of God. He has observed in intricate and total detail the workings and thought of every age and every culture. He is above the constraints of human culture and of the limitations that religious belief systems vainly seek to impose on the Almighty. The dream was a look at human society from God's higher viewpoint. Through the imagery of that revelation God caused me to see the captivity and bondage of man to man's own human system of thought and behavior that form the boundaries of 'normal' human existence. The crisscross track work of the dream is closely akin to the "veil which is woven over all nations" that God has promised to swallow up. This human system of thought and action forms the boundaries within which human life is normally lived in this world. (Isaiah 25:7)

A fact unknown to the masses bound to this system is that all of it serves the interest and is under the direct supervision and power of a higher dominating intelligence - revealed in the Bible to be the rebel spirit known as satan. Most people would scoff to think that satan had a metal shackle around their neck and had them chained to his instrument of slavery. That is, of course, the ignorance revealed in the revelation. How blinded they are to their own pitiful condition!

The next surprising feature of the dream was the man who appeared seemingly out of nowhere to remove the spikes that held the wretched system in place and to use those very spikes to pierce the head of the diabolical overlord. Who could this be except the Man who came from Heaven and removed those wretched spikes labeled 'sin' and 'death' by allowing them to be driven through his own human flesh?! In this beautiful self-sacrificing act the Son of God set the human creation free of satan's bondage while inflicting a critical blow to the head of the enemy. How tragic that the slaves of satan's system have not grasped the truth that they have been set free. Life chained to the metal tracks is all they know. Not being willing to seize the freedom they have been given they continue to live out their lives in futile servitude to the bondage of men.

How About You?

How about you? Do you begin to feel the weight of the chain and shackle around your neck? I hope so. For, make no mistake, a time is fast approaching when the victorious Messiah will return to finish the work he has started - to obliterate the system of human slavery and to permanently dethrone its' invisible ruler. Are you saying, "I'm a Christian. I'm saved. This doesn't apply to me. It applies to the world. They are the ones with the shackles—not me." If that is your reaction then I caution you that such a feeling of relief is probably premature—as will be demonstrated farther along in this work.

It Changed My Life

I have just outlined 'the big picture' of the meaning of the dream as it affects us all. As for the remainder of the dream—it is personal. This indicates the call of God on my life and the things I was destined to suffer in answering that call. I have been called to bear witness to the captivity that God has revealed to me and to point the way to and to fight for every individual soul within my sphere of action who seeks to be free. The call on my life is to be God's instrument of freedom to those who will hear me. The final haunting image of the dream, namely, the indecision of my wife as to which direction she would go, indicated something that, although plain enough, I had not wanted to see. Namely, that my answering God's call could result in great personal loss to myself—even including the possible loss of my beloved wife and our family together. Alas, these years of ministry since the calling of God have brought me to a place of great loss and great gain. That God has restored losses to me makes them no less meaningful. The system will not let real freedom go unpunished. The price must be so high that no one will dare to choose freedom. That is part of the mechanism that keeps us all slaves. Nevertheless, you can be free—but only if you are willing to pay the price. Indeed, at such a high price my freedom is very dear to me. The freedom that has been purchased through my loss is this: Having nothing left within the system to claim my heart I am free to tell the truth.

The brief explanation of the shackle dream that I have just presented is an understanding that I have arrived at over time. I did not have benefit of this understanding at the time this revelation was dropped upon me out of heaven. It was simply and suddenly there like a giant obstruction dropped in my path that I was forced to deal with. My first interpretation of the dream was, of course, concerned with my immediate situation; but the effect of the dream was to leave me stunned and wondering what God wanted from me. After wrestling with this for three days, I arrived at a crucial point of decision. I was scared and I knew from the dream that accepting God's call could mean the loss of my whole world. It was a call to total surrender of the caliber described by the apostle, Paul; "...The time has been shortened, so that from now on both those who have wives should be as though they had none; and those who weep, as though they did not weep; and those who rejoice as though they did not rejoice; and those who buy, as though they did not possess; and those who use the world, as though they did not make full use of it; for the form of this world is passing away." (1 Corinthians 7:29-31)

I loved my wife, my family, my friends and my things as much as anyone does. But for some reason that I couldn't understand God was calling on me to give Him and His cause the urgent first priority in my life. I found God's call to freedom and service irresistibly compelling. In my bed, on the night of February 6, 1981, I gave God my answer in prayer.

Another Encounter

My prayer began something like this, "God, I am really scared; I know you are calling me to something—but I am not sure what it exactly is. I know if I follow you I could lose everything. I am afraid

I am not good enough or strong enough to do what you want—but if you will just be there to help me I am willing to do your will, whatever it is."

At about that point my mind was filled with a strange vision. The effect was very much like being in a dark room and suddenly having a 360-degree movie switched on. It was really like being instantly transported into another place. You could say it was like a dream, only I was completely awake at the time. [What you just read is how I described this event years ago. Describing it now, I could say that experience was something like the concept of virtual reality. Of course, in early 1981 when I had the vision that term or the concept behind it did not yet exist.] What I saw was a vast flat arid plane stretching off in every direction as far as I could see. Once again the ground was sand, dead sand. The only shapes breaking up the flat endless field of sand were some kind of strange large stones scattered endlessly across the surface. They were hard to make out because they were partially buried under the sand and many of them had dried-up vegetation growing up around them. As my gaze took in the randomly scattered and obscured stones I noticed that they were more than simply rocks. I could make out that they were cut stones, despite the sand and the vegetation obscuring my view. I wondered what I was seeing. Suddenly my heart was pierced with the words, "This is the Temple of God."

The tragedy that those words signified went through my heart like an arrow and I began to bitterly sob with sadness that came upon me out of heaven. I believe what I experienced was God's own heartbreak over the broken down and scattered condition of His desolate Temple. I also felt convicted and guilty knowing that I had contributed to the breakdown of God's own House. The sense of conviction was so great; but I was trapped in this vision with no place to run away to and no place to hide. I instinctively cried out for the only relief possible in the best words I could muster at the time; "Lord Jesus, please speak for me in heaven." As I spoke those words my spirit actually saw the Son of God go before the Father. Before I could even finish the sentence the deed was done. It was like He had just been standing there eagerly waiting for me to make the needed request so that before I could even finish making it He had acted.

The Work Of The Holy Spirit

Everything changed instantly as His Spirit was poured out upon me and into me. My whole being was filled with a warm sense of complete and utter acceptance, love and security. In that moment I knew I was a son of God. I delighted in the ecstasy of what was happening to me. I quite literally was being baptized in the Holy Spirit. I could feel the Spirit all around me, even under me, as if lifting me off the bed. The Spirit was soaking into me, into my body and my spirit as if I were a dried out sponge. Even while this was happening my mind was being quickened and flooded with Scriptures coming back from my memory - dropping into place as if they were pieces of some giant puzzle. Suddenly I just knew things that I had never known before! This was at once my adoption into the family of God and my anointing for the service for which I had been called. I was a new man with a new life and my parting with the old life was as certain and complete as if I had died and had been buried. The fact is, in a spiritual sense I had died and been buried—and been resurrected and empowered for a new life hidden with Messiah in God.

Much has happened in the years since that initial encounter of my ministry. But my purpose here is not to try to impress you with stories of supernatural events or to try to justify an admittedly strange and unusual life. This is not intended to be an autobiography. I am sharing this experience with you because what I hope to impart is something of the heart of God even as He has imparted it to me. I believe that the revelations that I have just described are an important communication with God expressing His deepest concern in this hour. For that reason we, His sons, must care as He cares. We must open up our hearts to understand the depths of His concern and we must give ourselves wholly and completely to the task of giving Him His heart's desire. This may be a different way for you to think about God. Perhaps like so many, you usually think about God in the context of what He can do for you. It is time to stop being so selfish. Our loving Father needs us. That is not a typo. If it seems like one to you then read on.

The Temple Tragedy

As we consider the scattered Temple vision certain questions present themselves. What does this mean? What are the stones? Why does God see them as scattered and overgrown? What is the relationship of this vision to the earlier dream? The general meaning of the vision is simple to anyone with the most basic knowledge of Scripture. God's Temple is His corporate people. Not an actual stone building but a spiritual building made up of living stones called by God to that purpose. As Peter wrote; "You also, as living stones, are being built up as a spiritual house for a holy priesthood, to offer up spiritual sacrifices acceptable to God through Y'shua the Messiah." (1 Peter 2:5)

The immense tragedy that the vision depicts is that those living stones are not being built into a spiritual house for God as they were intended to be. Instead, they are shown to be rather dead, scattered and overgrown and obscured by sand and weeds. This is a desolate and heartbreaking picture indeed. Are things really that bad? If so, how did things get this way? How can they change?

Sharing The Fruits Of My Decades Of Struggle

For decades I have struggled with the immensity of what God has laid upon me. Often, I have made a fool of myself trying to do what it seemed my call indicated. I have just as often been blessed with supernatural success when I would forget myself and just let God use me as a vessel through which to act. Allowing myself to be used as a vessel has also made me look like a fool, but at least in that instance I am comforted in the knowledge that I am a fool for my Lord. Only after all this experiential struggle, and having chewed on all this under the guiding hand of the Holy Spirit for these many years, have I come to the place where I can fully share the meaning of God's revelation with those who will receive it. We must begin by looking in greater depth at the shackle dream.

The principal features of the shackle dream that became most immediately obvious were these: First, the immense track network that forms the oppressive framework within which all human activity takes place, and second, the overlord of it all, unseen by the masses below but exercising seemingly unquestioned dominion just the same. Certain questions that immediately come to mind are these:

How did mankind come into slavery to the track-work system? Indeed, where did it come from in the first place? And how did the overlord come to be in authority over the world system? Perhaps the most puzzling question is this one: If not the world system then what else is there? To answer these basic questions we must look back to the time before the world system was established—before the enemy had established his oppressive authority over mankind. In our quest for understanding we must go back eons before the beginning of time itself—before the very beginning of God's creation—and move forward from there.

2

THE BEDROCK OF CREATION

About two thousand years ago our earth was visited by its Maker. By the most amazing miracle of all time He emptied Himself of His heavenly glory to be born into this world as one of us. He is, of course, known to many as Jesus of Nazareth and to some of us as Lord Jesus Christ and yet to others of us as our Lord, Y'shua the Messiah. It is to those who truly know Him as Lord that I am mainly writing, regardless of how they may presently say His Name. All we know or hope to know about what went on before time must come through Him. Indeed, a primary reason why He came was to reveal the hidden things of God to those destined to become God's sons. At this point we will see what we can glean about pre-creation realities from His revelation. (Philippians 2:5-11)

The Word - The Revelation Of God

In point of fact, He was and is the revelation. Perhaps that is why He never used his precious time on earth to write a book for us. Instead He lived intimately with a few chosen men to whom He imparted His own life through simply being Who He is. It was difficult for those men to abide His presence, for they were men like us with minds shackled to the ways of this world while He was the very embodiment of a higher life. So often their earthbound thinking brought them into conflict with His seemingly inscrutable ways and words. He was never in the slightest danger of becoming like them. He was not moved by 'peer pressure' or social pressures of any kind. He would be Who He would be. However, in course of time those men were thoroughly and completely changed by His presence. The duty of passing on the Truth they saw in Him and heard from Him fell to them. It is to them and other chosen contemporaries of theirs that we must look for the accurate record of His revelation during His visit to this world. (John 1:14)

Speaking for that original group of apostles (sent ones, emissaries) who lived with Y'shua, the apostle, John wrote: "It was there from the beginning: we have heard it; we have seen it with our eyes; we looked upon it, and felt it with our hands; and it is of this we tell. Our theme is the word of life [or Word of Life]. This life [or Life] was made visible; we have seen it and bear our testimony; we here declare to you the eternal life [or Eternal Life] which dwelt with the Father and was made visible to us. What we have seen and heard we declare to you, so that you and we together may share in a common life, that life which we share with the Father and his Son Jesus Christ. And we write this in order that the joy of us all may be complete." The Hebrew Names Version concludes it this way; "our fellowship is with the Father, and with his Son, Yeshua the Messiah. And we write these things to you, that our joy may be fulfilled." (1 John 1:1-4 NEB, brackets mine)

Translators have some difficulty translating these words from the original Greek. Unlike English the ancient Koine Greek does not distinguish proper nouns, including names and titles, by the use of capital letters. The context must determine capitalization and punctuation for translation into English. The problem for the translator is the impersonal "it" used by the writer while obviously referring to his experience with the Person, "Jesus Christ." This presents the translator with a conundrum. Should it be word of life or Word of Life, life or Life, eternal life or Eternal Life? The impersonal "it" suggests that the writer is talking about something other than a person while the context [we have...seen...heard...felt...was made visible...dwelt with the Father] suggests a person.

The only logical conclusion is that the writer meant what he wrote. He identifies the "Word of Life" so closely with Y'shua that they must be considered one and the same. At the same time his words suggest a certain "it," a certain something, specifically, a certain 'life' he experienced in Y'shua that was larger than the human being that had embodied that 'life.' "It [the Word of Life] was from the beginning" and was "eternal life" while the man, Y'shua, had a definite birth and death. The writer is so bold as to offer a sharing in that common life to his readers, calling it, according to the NEB, "that life which we share with the Father and his Son Jesus Christ."

Eyewitness Testimony

This, then is our starting place. Testimony from one who personally knew the Son of God as a man on earth. Testimony from one who, through association with Him, actually entered into the common life originally shared only by "the Father and his Son Yeshua the Messiah." This apostle puts the emphasis on that unique common life of the Father and the Son as the very purpose of his testimony. We find his story of the Life in the Gospel of John. Dear brother, look now at that testimony with new, fresh, eyes.

"When all things began, The Word already was. The Word dwelt with God, and what God was, the Word was. The Word, then, was with God at the beginning, and through him all things came to be; no single thing was created without him." (John 1:1-3 NEB)

The One identified as The Word of Life in 1 John 1:1 is similarly referred to here as The Word. Before creation, before a single thing was ever made, The Word already existed. However, He did not exist alone. He dwelt with God. What God was He was. He shared the same God-nature and life as Father God while also enjoying individual Personhood so as to dwell with God. Only individuals can share, can fellowship, can exist in relationship to each other. God is a Person, as is The Word. What then is the relationship between the Two that John is unfolding before us? John makes the point clearly in his conclusion to this thought regarding The Word in John 1:18: "No one has ever seen God; but God's only Son, he who is nearest to the Father's heart, he has made him known." (John 1:18 NEB)

The God Family

The relationship is clear. Father God is one party. "God's only Son," earlier identified as The Word, is the other party. They dwelt together. They shared the same nature and the same life. Friends, we commonly call this kind of relationship a family. This is the God Family, the First Family existent from before all creation. That is the clear meaning of John's words in calling them Father and Son. Perhaps we shy away from drawing this obvious conclusion because we think of a family as a human thing and consider it irreverent to apply the term to God. We would do well to raise our thinking a few notches to realize that all families, no matter how imperfect, take their pattern from the First Family (Should not those created in God's image reflect God's nature and ways?).

Any family is a unity of a sort while also being made up of individuals sharing in a common life. The First Family is infinitely more so. We can only begin to imagine the untold eternity that these Two shared together as all that was, perfect and complete in their fellowship with one another. Father to Son - Son to Father - United in One Spirit - fully occupied with nothing else but loving each other as the fullness of all then existing. words fail the thought. This is a unity and a fellowship beyond the imagination of mere created beings. No wonder God's only, in the sense of, unique, Son should be called "the Word." Who else has this same eternal ground of experience and shared life and nature in fellowship with the Father so as to make Him known to all creation? Only the One Who has experienced all creation and pre-creation with the Father, "he who is nearest to the Father's heart," could be called The Word of God. Compared to Him no one knows God at all.

The Son Reveals The Father

With this background in mind the claims of Y'shua that were considered so outrageous by His religious contemporaries come into focus as simply the factual truth: "I am the way and the truth and the life. No one comes to the Father except through me. If you really knew me, you would know my Father as well... Believe me when I say that I am in the Father and the Father is in me." (John 14:6,7,11)

Understanding then that the Son is the highest possible source of enlightenment about His own relationship with His Father. let us see what He reveals about the nature of that relationship.

In the Gospel of John alone the term "Father" is used sixty-two times. In the vast majority of those times Y'shua is referring to God as His Father and as THE Father. This is no mere religious title. The Son used the term Father because it best identifies the Person He was talking about. What the Son considered essentially characteristic of that Individual so as to identify Him to us is summed up in the word, Father. So much so, in fact, that God by his very nature is THE Father, that is, the model and source of fatherhood itself.

The Son Personifies Sonship

Correspondingly, Y'shua refers to Himself as the Son. There are thirty-eight references to the word son in the Gospel of John alone. In most of these Y'shua refers to Himself as THE Son. He is the model and source of sonship itself. His essential nature is that of The Son.

What we see here is that Fatherhood and Sonship were not concepts that were created. Rather, they existed in the very nature of the Father and the Son from before the beginning of creation. This is the bedrock of the relationship out of which all creation was brought into being. Stop and let the prodigious weight of this truth sink in.

What Fatherhood And Sonship Are All About

How then does Y'shua describe the respective roles of Father and Son in the Divine Family? The nature of fatherhood is to be the source of life while sonship defines the product and expression of that life. Consistent with that, the Son declares: "...I live because of the Father." (John 6:57)

He also states: "As the Father has life in himself, so he has granted the Son to have life in himself." (John 5:26)

In those statements the Son acknowledges life as granted to Him by His Father. John calls Him the Only Begotten Son and the Son uses that same term to describe Himself. As the Only Begotten Son He is begotten of His Father's own life rather than having been made as a created being. (John 1:14, 18; 3:16,18)

An Eternal Being

These statements need not be interpreted to mean that the Son had a beginning. Since the Father existed from the eternal past without a beginning His begettal of the Son could also be without a beginning. If "what God was the Word was," that is, if the Word uniquely shares the same God nature as the Father, then it would seem to follow that He too is an eternal being without a beginning. The unchangeable nature of God as Father would also seem to force this conclusion, since one must have a child to be a father. Let us acknowledge humbly that we are talking here about things that transcend human experience and thought. Only the Father and the Son experientially know of what we speak.

What We Share With The First Family

Though much, if not most, of the reality of the pre-creation Family is beyond human grasp let us take heart in the fact that we also have certain essentials in common with that Family. For example, we should all know that the primary motivation in any family should be love. Notice that is the pattern in the First Family: "For the Father loves the Son and shows him all that he does." (John 5:20)

For the Father love means drawing His Son into fellowship wherein He shares all of Himself and his work with His Son. Love is expressed toward the Father by eagerly receiving from Him, but more than that, through obeying Him. The Son put it this way; "... I love the Father and I do exactly what my Father has commanded me." "I do nothing on my own but speak just what the Father has taught me." (John 14:31, 8:28)

Love, Authority And Respect In God's Order

This brings us to another fundamental feature of the Father-Son relationship that is not beyond our grasp. That feature is order of authority and respect. In this department the Son leaves no doubt as to Who has the highest authority in the First Family; "the Father is greater than I," He declares. (John 14:28)

As the perfect Son He can state categorically "I honor my Father." (John 8:49)

Notice how love, Fatherhood authority, and respectful obedience inherent to true Sonship form the principle of operation, the divine order, within the First Family. The perfect love of the Father puts His every command beyond question as being for the ultimate good of His Loved One. Absolute obedience from a willing heart is the only fitting response of true Sonship. "...I love the Father and I do exactly what my Father has commanded me."

Submission From A Willing Heart

It is interesting that some would seek to relieve the Son of the need for obedience to the Father. They would suggest that since the Son is also God, sharing the same divine nature as the Father, He must also be equal in intrinsic authority to the Father. Since, in their thinking, obedience to the Father would make the Son less than the Father they find themselves in the strange position of denying a fundamental truth that Y'shua reiterated on numerous occasions; namely, that He is flawlessly obedient to His Father. Their thinking would strip the Son of His very reason for being.

The failure of such thinking probably lies in the mistaken and sinful notion that all submission is oppressive. Let's face it: humans, modern humans especially, hate to obey anybody. It is considered demeaning and humiliating. Authority expressed in love with a corresponding submission motivated by love is not something we easily grasp. In this we are very unlike God. Both authority and submission motivated by love are revealed by the Word as essential to the Divine Nature. The Son has revealed Himself to be equal in nature to His Father. He has also revealed the Father as being His Source of life and greater in authority within the First Family. His submission to the Father is not oppressive because it is not forced. It is the willing expression of the Son's own heart. It is natural to the relationship. This is what Fatherhood/Sonship is all about.

The truth is: the Son looks to the Father as the Source of all things and therefore calls Him "My God" and "the only true God" (John 20:17; 17:3)

He says the Father is the source of His life, His knowledge, and His work. Even the Holy Spirit "issues from the Father" (John 6:57; 8:28; 5:36; 15:26 NEB).

Don't Be Stupid

At this point we must momentarily depart from our theme with this warning: Let us not get stupid here and attempt to use these facts to diminish the Son's authority over us. What we are looking into is the intimate relationship within the God Family. This is a gracious glimpse into the private lives of God and His Son! This is a look at the order inherent within their relationship between themselves. Let us not presumptuously assert that because we see an aspect of that private relationship that we can make a division between the authority of the Father and the Son as respects ourselves. When the authority of God is projected beyond the bounds of the First Family toward us it has equal force whether from the Father directly or from the Son. This is so because, as we have already read, the Son does nothing but the Father's will. (John 14:31, 8:28, etc.)

The Son's Authority

Further, the Son is so completely at unity with the Father, sharing His life and His nature, molded to the Father through an eternity of fellowship with Him, that they are "one."

"I and the Father are one....Anyone who has seen me has seen the Father. Don't you believe that I am in the Father, and that the Father is in me? The words I say to you are not just my own. Rather, it is the Father, living in me, who is doing his work." (John 10:30, 14:9-10)

What this means for all created beings, ourselves included, is that the Son is Head over all things to us and is to be honored and obeyed equally with the Father. To honor Him is to honor God. He is our Maker. He is, in fact, also our only Judge. (John 1:1-3)

"Moreover, the Father judges no one, but has entrusted all judgment to the Son, that all may honor the Son just as they honor the Father. He who does not honor the Son does not honor the Father, who sent him." (John 5:22-23)

The testimony of John the Babtizer (Yochanan the Immerser) confirms this; "The Father loves the Son and has placed everything in his hands." (John 3:35)

Fittingly then, showing His rightful place as Head over all, the Son can say; "All that belongs to the Father is mine." (John 16:15)

Let us be silent then, and bend our knee before the awesome glory of the Lord!

The First Patriarchal Family?

Having acknowledged our Lord's claim to our hearts and our obedience let us return to our present theme: the pre-creation relationship of the Father and the Son. Let us acknowledge that since that relationship issues forth from the very nature of God and His Son, and God does not change, the essential nature of that relationship must remain eternally the same. How could we best describe that God Family relationship?

What the Son of God reveals is unquestionably a Patriarchal Family as described by the Merriam-Webster Dictionary definition for "patriarchy." That is; "social organization marked by the supremacy of the father in the clan or family."

This truth may be hard for some to accept in this feminist age but it is nonetheless true. Y'shua revealed God as FATHER, not Mother, or even Parent—He is THE FATHER. There is no instance anywhere in Scripture that represents God as being feminine—despite modern attempts to mitigate the hard edge of that fact. Likewise, the Word is revealed to be The Son, not Daughter, or even Child—He is THE SON. As the Firstborn Son (in the sense of preeminent rather than literally born) He is the rightful Heir of all that belongs to His Father. "All that belongs to the Father is mine" He declares. Being in a pure Patriarchal Family He is endowed with authority from His Father over all the Family holdings—in this case the entire created universe! The apostle Paul makes exactly the same point regarding the Son: "He is the image of the invisible God, the firstborn over all creation. For by him all things were created: things in heaven and on earth, visible and invisible...all things were created by [lit. through] him and for him. He is before all things, and in him all things hold together." (Colossians 1:15-17)

Do you get the import of this? The universe was created in a Patriarchal Family context!

At Odds With The Gentile Doctrine Of God

If you observed that this revelation varies in emphasis from the normal regurgitation of the trinity doctrine you are quite correct. Let me tell you briefly here why that is: Over thousands of years God carefully created and groomed the Hebrew culture, imperfect though it was, to provide the context in which the Son of God would reveal His glory. As a patriarchal society they understood the meaning and true implications of Messiah's claim to be the Son of God as well as His claims regarding the Father. His claims were much too grand for most to accept, but at least they were rejecting something that they understood. This was so because they lived every day, though imperfectly, within the context of patriarchal family life.

Now fast-forward about 300 years from the time of Messiah's death to 325 A.D. A pagan Roman emperor, Constantine, is experiencing discord in his kingdom. By then the "Christianity" of the first century had largely degenerated into a gentile religion patterned much more after the world around them than after Christ (the word 'Christ' is from the Greek equivalent of the Hebrew word for 'Messiah'). I say a gentile religion because nearly everything Hebraic was then looked upon with an air of superiority and disgust from the Roman perspective. Greek and Roman philosophy and the ancient mystery religions dominated the thinking of the day and so dominated the thinking within the Christian religion. The nature of Christ was being debated in that atmosphere and the result was confusion and dissension in the Christian religion, and therefore in Constantine's empire.

The pagan emperor of Rome reacted by calling a council of "Catholic" (Universal) leaders to decide this issue. Any who were loyal to the Headship of Christ stayed home, of course, rather than concede such power over His Body to an earthly authority. The rest who showed up hammered out the first draft of the trinity doctrine in a political fiasco not unlike the political wrangling of Congress or any other bureaucratic body. It is doubtful that there was a Hebraic believer in the bunch. It is doubtful that a single participant was there who understood Y'shua's words in the context in which He spoke them. Given these circumstances and the Greek philosophy that ruled the day is it any wonder that they came up with a confusing formula for God that even now cannot be understood?

That is not to say that there is nothing good in the trinity doctrine, so far as it goes. Yet, it clearly misses the patriarchal truth so clearly revealed by the Son and found in the Gospels. The very idea of reducing the infinite God to a doctrinal formula trivializes Him. It is blasphemous, to say the least, for humans to even attempt such a thing! That is why no such formula exists in the Scriptures. Instead, the Scriptures give us all of God's history with man, as well as God in Messiah Himself to reveal the Father to us.

It is amazing that countless Christians over centuries of time have continued to impose this man-made doctrinal matrix over the clear revelation of the Son of God. It's long past time to throw out this man-made dogma and listen to the revelation of Y'shua in the context in which it was given.

What was that context? The context of Hebraic tribal society.

That brings us back to our point: After an eternity of fellowship together the Ultimate Patriarch (lit, father-ruler: "patri"=father and "arch"=ruler) created the universe with, through and for His Son, Whom He also put in charge of it all. The Father created the universe with a specific plan in mind. That plan was meant to unfold - is unfolding - fashioned in perfect order consistent with God's own patriarchal nature. It is very safe to say that loving patriarchal order is the highest sort of order in the universe—it is the Divine order.

The implications of this for God's men and families are nothing less than universal!

FOOTNOTES:

On reading this chapter some have asked; what of the Holy Spirit? Our emphasis here is on the Father and the Son. The role of the Holy Spirit will come more into play as we proceed. However, at this point we can say that the Holy Spirit does play a role totally consistent with what is revealed above. The comment below, defending the view of the Western Church regarding the Filioque Clause of the Nicene Creed (namely, that the Spirit proceeds from the Father and the Son), very nicely expresses the role of the Holy Spirit from before Creation:

"Thus, if anyone asks what is the special activity of the Holy Spirit, we must answer that it is to unite in love. And if it is of the nature of the Spirit to unite things, then we may be sure that He has been carrying out this activity for all eternity. Before there was a Church, before there was physical life of any kind, the Spirit was the bond of love and unity between the Father and the Son. From all eternity, independently of any created being, God is the Lover, the Loved, and the Love itself. And the bond of unity and love that exists between the Father and the Son proceeds from the Father and the Son." (From: The Filioque Clause, an Appendix to Creed Nicene, Posted by: James E. Kiefer, Source: CHRISTIA File Archives, INDEX CHRISTIA, listserv@asuvm.inre.asu.edu)

3

GOD'S ORDER ESTABLISHED

Consider the implications of the patriarchal context in which the universe was created as we review God's creative work. As we have just seen, before God created anything he existed in beautiful united fellowship with his Son, the Logos, the Word. That full revelation had to wait for the coming of God's Son to earth. Thus Genesis does not concern itself with the eternal past. With a huge brush stroke the first verse of the Bible covers all God's creative work from its start through the earth's preparation for man. "In the beginning God created the heavens and the earth." (John 1:1, Genesis 1:1)

God created the heavens first so let us begin with the heavens also. Broadly speaking, the Bible reveals that there are three heavens. The first, and the one most familiar to humans is the actual physical heaven comprised of our atmosphere and infinitely beyond into space. The third is the Realm wherein God Himself dwells. The Apostle Paul in some way was privileged to pass beyond the first and second heaven to enter into the third heaven where he learned things that he could not even repeat. Between the physical heaven and the highest heaven is mid-heaven. It is the vast spiritual realm created to be the domain of spirit life and is itself divided into ascending levels of glory. (2 Corinthians 12:2-4, Revelation 14:6)

Through the Son, God created various forms of spirit life to occupy the spiritual realms he had created. Since spirits do not reproduce, each one was individually created to carry out certain assigned duties within God's unfolding plan. They are not all the same even though we generally refer to all of them as angels, literally meaning 'messengers.' Angels have intellect and power surpassing man, and like man, have free moral agency as individuals. As such they have personal names such as Michael and Gabriel as two examples. God created a finite but huge number of angels, "myriads of myriads" of them. (John 1:1-3, Matthew 22:30)

Forms Of Angelic Life

There are two distinct forms of angelic life named in the Bible. Seraphim are always shown as ministering at God's throne in heaven, ever worshiping Him and voicing unceasing praise of His majestic glory and holiness. The Hebrew word Seraphim literally means "burning ones," referring, no doubt, to their burning passion for God's holiness, displayed in their constant worship in the Divine Presence. The other revealed form of angelic life are the Cherubim.

In contrast to the Seraphim, who are constantly attendant upon The Divine Majesty in the highest heaven, the Cherubim are designed to be agents of God's glory and Sovereign Will throughout the visible and unseen universe. The Creator is said to "sit above the Cherubim." (Isaiah 6:1-3, 1 Samuel 4:4, 2 Samuel 2:6, 2 Kings 19:15, 1 Chronicles 13:6, Psalms 80:1, 99:1, Isaiah 37:16)

They are described as being one and the same as God's 'chariot.' God is spoken of as 'riding' on them - all descriptive of their function as God's agents in implementing the Divine Will as God directs. (1 Chronicles 28:18, 2 Samuel 22:11, Psalms 18:10)

When you think of "Cherubs" think not of cute, baby-like creatures with wings. That is not the Biblical picture. On the contrary, these creatures have always appeared to humans in a form resembling impressive grown men. Just one of these beings killed 185,000 soldiers in one night! Apparently, one of the abilities God gave to angels at their creation is the ability to assume a materialized manlike form, though that was never intended to be their usual state of being. This would be useful to God as He could then send angels among men as messengers of His as He would see fit. There are numerous instances recorded in Scripture where such materialized angels (probably all Cherubim) appeared to humans.

The Nature Of Angelic Authority

At their respective individual creation each angelic son of God was given specific authority, intrinsic to their being, and appropriate to their intended station and function. At the very top of the Angelic order is the rank of 'Archangel,' with Michael being the only such angel mentioned by name in the Bible. However, in Daniel 10:13 (NAS) Michael is spoken of as being "one of the chief princes," indicating that there are others of similar high rank as well. The point here is that the individually created angels were created to function within a hierarchical system, that is, within a fixed chain of command. However, this is not a big bureaucratic machine after the manner of human hierarchical governments so familiar to our modern world. The difference is this: "To where the spirit (God's Spirit) was to go, there they (the Cherubim) went, they did not turn in their going." (Ezekiel 1:12, Jude 9).

Yes, it is the Holy Spirit, present everywhere and aware of everything always, imparting life and direction to the angelic order, anticipating and managing every need even before it arises, that makes the crucial difference. This Personal involvement of the all-knowing and all-powerful One enables God's heavenly angelic host to work in perfect harmony without the flaws and bureaucratic death of a Spiritless system.

All Authority Originates In God

Let's consider how all this relates to the matter of authority. God, by virtue of His Creatorship and Godhood, rightfully has absolute sovereignty over all His creation. He created it, so it is all His to do with as He wishes. Correspondingly, it is the unequivocal obligation of His creation to be and do what God, the Creator, intends and directs. This is the most basic principle of life; the "prime directive," if you will. Since God is before all others and has sovereignty over all others then it stands to reason that all authority originates in Him. As we have seen, the scriptures further indicate that this authority of God is invested in the Son and is expressed through and by Him.

Authority First Delegated Through The Son To Angels

God's authority was first delegated to intelligent creatures when God, through the Son, created angels. The authority of each angel is intrinsic to its specific abilities and intended function and is an individual reflection of God's own authority and glory. Understand that there is no authority except by God. Through His Son He is the Creator of all authority, originating with the various levels of angelic glories. Paul explains it like this: "For in Him ["God's beloved Son" verse 13] all things were created, both in the heavens and on earth, visible and invisible, whether thrones or dominions or rulers or authorities—all things have been created through Him and for Him. And He is before all things, and in Him all things hold together." (Colossians 1:16-17 NAS, Romans 13:1)

Our Loving Father Prepares A Home For Man

Once God had completed the invisible spirit creation He set about doing a new work much to the amazement and delight of His heavenly family. The angels were there to observe and be moved to worship by God's masterful creation of the physical universe. As stars occupy our physical heaven, angels occupy the spirit heaven. For that reason these heavenly sons of God are often spoken of as "stars" in the Bible. God tells of their reaction to His creation of the earth: "Where were you when I (God) laid the foundation of the earth? ...When the morning stars sang together, And all the sons of God shouted for joy?" (Job 38:4,7)

The "morning stars", the angelic "sons of God" observed how God systematically formed and prepared one tiny speck of His created universe for a special purpose. That speck we refer to as the earth.

The preparations that God made here were for His crowning achievement—the creation of man. God's final preparation was the creation of a beautiful garden paradise. It was large, with four major rivers having headwaters there, in the Mesopotamian Valley in the area of the world that we now refer to as Iraq. That garden area was filled with all kinds of delicious and wholesome fruit and vegetation, both as a source of food and natural beauty to satisfy the man. God had previously created many different kinds of animal life and these were present in pleasing variety and abundance within the garden. This natural first home of man is referred to in the Bible as the Garden of Eden. It was a wonderful place. It never rained there. A gentle mist came up from the ground to water the vegetation. It was a perfect, comfortable, safe and secure home just waiting for the creation of its lord, namely, man.

Father God Works His Will Through Life And Growth

Let us pause a moment to learn about our Creator and His ways. Notice here God's way of dealing and working with man. The nature of God is to work through the organic expression of life that he originated. The natural world that God gave man as his domain expresses God's organic way of working. Each living thing that God created, from vegetation to fish, birds, animals and man - all were created with the re-creative power within themselves to reproduce "after their kind." Each carried within its seed a living blueprint from God's own mind that, through the miracle of life from God, would grow into the mature living creation that God had envisioned. For example, when God created plant life: "God said, Let the earth cause grass to spring up, herb producing seed, fruit-trees yielding fruit after their kind, the seed of which is in them, on the earth. And it was so." (Genesis 1:11 Darby)

So we see each living thing has the divine imprint of its own purpose and identity within its seed. Beyond that, all earthly life is interconnected and interdependent according to a higher plan that unfolds into reality through the growth of the creative life within all living things. God brought this symphony of life together in a wonderful way to form a 'womb' for the beginnings of mankind - namely, the Garden of Eden. Although the Garden of Eden seems too simple and idyllic for modern man to consider as more than a myth, its very nature reflects God's way of doing things. There were no buildings, machines, forms to fill out, records to keep, or bureaucracies to bow down to in the Garden. For that matter, there weren't even any clothes! Everything there was natural and alive. Here we have a fundamental principle established that we need to remember: God works out His Will for man through the organic expression of life. What we are talking about here is life and growth working out the will of the Creator. We will expand on this theme as we progress.

The Father's Love Manifest From The Beginning Toward Man

Let this important fact also not escape our notice: God is full of love and grace that must be expressed. The careful preparations and provisions that God had made in all that he created for the man and his offspring testify eloquently to the perfect love of God's heart motivating His liberal generosity and creativity. The nature of that love was that of grace. Grace is unearned favor, poured out freely as an expression of the love of the Giver rather than as something owed to the receiver. Adam was nothing but a clump of dust when God created the earth for him! He had never done a thing to earn it. What works could he possibly do to earn it? God's grace is the love of a Father Who delights in giving good gifts to His children. They continue to receive of His grace simply through trusting their Father and remaining in vital relationship with Him. Such is the generous nature of God's love. Such are the riches of those in the family of God!

After all these loving preparations had been made, the time finally came for God to create the object of all of this love and affection that he had so liberally poured out into his natural creation. Speaking to His Beloved Son and Fellow-Worker: "God said, "Let Us make man in Our Image, according to Our likeness; and let them rule over the fish of the sea...the birds...the cattle...and over all the earth." And God created man in His own image, in the image of God He created him; male and female He created them. And God blessed them; and God said to them, Be fruitful and multiply...and rule." (Genesis 1:26-28)

The Difference Between Men And Angels

It is instructive to compare this new order of intelligent creature, Man, with those spirits that God had already created in the spirit realm. The most obvious difference is that the man was designed to live in a physical body. Living as a physical being would enable the man to do something the angels were not intended to do— reproduce their own kind. Having a physical body would not mean that the man was just another animal. He would be created 'in God's image,' that is, with a spirit nature within that was created according to the likeness of God and His Son, perfectly reflecting God's own character. God's Spirit could thus 'tune in' to the spirit of man (and visa versa) to provide personal guidance and spiritual sustenance for the individual. This would enable God and man to enjoy fellowship with one another, since they would be like one another in character.

Man, Dominion And Natural Authority

Like the angels, man was given authority for his task. In man's case it would be authority to 'rule...over all the earth.' The word 'rule' is often seen as a harsh word these days. While being a strong word it is not meant to be a harsh word here. Many Bibles translate this word as "have dominion." To have dominion presents the idea of a specific area of responsibility to exercise authority over, which is the correct sense here. On earth Man was created to be lord in the image of God, reflecting God's own glory in the earth! The nature of man's authority was meant to be of a drastically different character than that of the angels. The angels, being individually created were given authority to perform within their place in a God-created hierarchical order. The man's authority would be 'in the image of God and His Son' - that is patriarchal family authority. The linking of the divine mandate to reproduce with dominion as noted above indicates that the authority that God gave the first man would be passed by natural reproduction to each new man born into the world. In a manner of speaking, each and every man would be a lord with the authority to rule over his own domain, but in direct submission to God. (Genesis 1:26-28)

The same life that produced a given individual would also be the force within him causing him to grow into the person he was meant to be—empowering him with full authority and freedom to be himself. In the sense of personal freedom then, no man would have greater authority than another because each would inherit the same authority first given to man. The only human authority that would exist over anyone would be that originating naturally in the family. That would be an authority of love and respect rather than oppression because it would be a natural family relationship. In God's perfect way there would be no human authority that was not personal, natural and motivated out of love.

An Expression Of Father God's Authority On Earth

This natural order of headship authority was meant to be an extension of God's own nature inherent in the relationship between the Father and the Son. The first man was created as an earthly son of God. As a son He was given the same authority originating in the Father. In God's image he was imbued with the same authority as that of his Creator—namely, fatherhood—patriarchal authority. Paul put it this way, "I bow my knees before the Father, from whom all fatherhood in heaven and on earth derives its name." God never did institute hierarchical authority on earth as He had in heaven among the angels. God instituted natural family authority on earth and it is as much an integral part of being human as expressing love, thinking or worshiping God. Much more about this will be revealed as we go on. How the unnatural bureaucratic forms of human authority came into the world will be explained later, also. At this point suffice it to say; they were not encompassed within God's original natural order for man. (Luke 3:38)

Created To Rule A Perfect Domain

The Bible tells us "Jehovah God formed the man out of dust from the ground, and blew into his nostrils the breath of life; and the man became a living soul." ["Jehovah" is one translated form of the Paleo-Hebrew YHWH which four-letter form we will be replacing back into the text from this point forward in this book.] It is interesting that this statement of the composition of man agrees with modern science, which has found that our bodies are composed from the elements of the earth. It is equally true that we are living souls because of the "breath of life" that animates us. Take away the breath and the life is soon to leave as well. (Genesis 2:7)

After He created the man "YHWH God took the man and put him into the Garden of Eden, to work it and to keep it." (Genesis 2:15)

Note here what rulership over the earth, beginning with the garden, entailed; "to work it and to keep it." Dominion over the earth is not a blank check to exploit, pillage and destroy. While it is true that God gave us the natural resources of the earth to use and enjoy it is equally true that the authority that God gave man over the earth was a sacred trust from God. To "rule over the earth" involves a responsibility to lovingly care for and preserve our earthly home and its resources in harmony with the natural order established by the Creator.

Let us leave thoughts of that weighty responsibility behind for the time being as we contemplate the first moments of life for the first of our kind. Imagine the first moments of the man, Adam, as he became aware. Imagine him looking around at his beautiful home, looking at and trying out parts of his perfectly formed and healthy human body ... being 'birthed' into existence in the presence and delighted fellowship of a loving heavenly Father.

Oh, how different was life for that first man from what it is today! The healthful and pleasant work of caring for his paradise home was meant to be a delight, not the daily struggle for survival that we are all too familiar with. In that blessed perfect state there was no cause for concern about corruption, chaos, or evil. Adam was created as a perfect man in the image of God. There was no evil in him or in the world around him. God had planted a special tree in the garden called the Tree of Life and Adam was allowed to eat from it freely along with an abundance of other fruit in the garden. That Tree of Life was there as a symbol for the man of the very fact that his life had God as its daily source and supply. So long as Adam was in fellowship with his loving heavenly Father, there was an endless life available to him. There was no worry about the physical corruption of his flesh - with that life from God the man could live forever. As for chaos intervening and cutting short the man's life, that too was not a worry. God assigned a powerful and high-ranking Cherub, to "cover" over the garden and prevent any accidental harm from coming to the man or his domain.

Danger In Paradise

Amid the perfection of fellowship and security that was Adam's home there was only one danger that the man needed to be concerned with. God warned the man of the danger so that it was unmistakably clear; "YHWH God commanded the man, saying, "You may freely eat of every tree in the garden ["every" would include the Tree of Life]; but of the Tree of Knowledge of Good and Evil you may not eat, for in the day that you eat of it, you shall surely die." (Genesis 2:16-17)

You may wonder why God would mar the beautiful paradise with the possibility of disaster for the man by creating that one deadly tree. It was simply God's way of providing the man something else he would need to live in the image of God - a choice. Without the actual possibility to choose something other than God and His ways the man would have been merely a fancy toy, a sort of living robot without real free will. Love is only real when it is expressed out of a free choice. For man to be made in the image of God he must be capable of real love. He must make the choice to love his Father for it to be real - for him to express true sonship. He must have a means of 'casting his vote' for something other than God for a choice of loving submission to God's sovereignty to be meaningful - hence the Tree of Knowledge of Good and Evil.

Two Trees = Two Ways

Actually, the two trees, the Tree of Life and the Tree of Knowledge of Good and Evil, represented to Adam the only two ways to live one's life. The Tree of Life was the way Adam was meant to live. Life was one and the same as perfect fellowship with God. Daily drawing his life from God in loving harmony with his Father and his Father's ways. It was the way of sonship. It was the way of faith, trust in God, Spirit to spirit. It was by grace. The Tree of Life offered no standard of good and evil that the man would have to live by. He simply would live as he had been created to live; trusting in God's love and expressing a heartfelt obedience to God's direction and the perfect mirror image of God's own character that was his own human spirit.

The Tree of Knowledge of Good and Evil was the alternative - independence from God. To eat that fruit was to say to God; "I don't need you. I'm going to live according to what seems right to me. I'm going to decide what's good or evil for myself." It was the only other choice. Since the man had free will that choice had to be available to the man. But God was not lying when He said it would result in death. The man was not God. He had no unending supply of life within himself. He needed to live in fellowship with God dependent on God for life. That's what he was made for. To disobey God, then, would be to break faith with his Source and could have no other result then the one God warned against, "You will surely die."

The Loving Father Anticipates Man's Every Need

Adam had no need to eat the forbidden fruit. He had plenty of other food to eat and a whole new world to explore and care for. And he had the enjoyment of daily fellowship with God as He would actually come and talk with the man in the Garden. After a suitable time for the man to get accustomed to life and his surroundings God took the next needed step. (Genesis 3:8-9)

"YHWH God said, It is not good, the man being alone. I will make a helper suited to him." (Genesis 2:18)

God saw this need before the man did. After all, he had physically and emotionally equipped the man for family life when he had created him. Before Adam would be ready, though, he would have to become aware of the need for a suitable companion for himself. God knew how to make the need obvious to Adam.

He gave Adam the job of naming all the animals in the Garden. This was an expression of man's rulership over his earthly kingdom so that "all which the man might call it, each living soul, that was its name." During observing all the different forms of animal life to appropriately name them Adam would note something common to them all—they all had mates. Yet, out of all those creatures there was no mate suitable for Adam. (Genesis 2:19)

Now that Adam was feeling the need for a companion/helper God acted in a beautiful way to fill that need:

God's Gift To Man

"YHWH God caused a deep sleep to fall on the man, and he slept. And He took one of his ribs, and closed up the flesh underneath. And YHWH God formed the rib which He had taken from the man into a woman, and brought her to the man. And the man said, "This now at last is bone of my bones, And flesh from my flesh. For this shall be called Woman, Because this has been taken out of Man." ...And they were both naked, the man and his woman, and were not ashamed." (Genesis 2:21-25)

True Marriage

Notice the beautiful simplicity of the first marriage. There was no need for some human institution and related mumbo-jumbo to "solemnize" the marriage. God made the woman from part of the man's own body. How could two people be any more 'married' than that? The marriage occurred when God brought the woman that He had created and selected for Adam and presented her to him and the man accepted her from God. On receiving his wife the man was so moved that he broke into the first poetry, accepting her as part of him - his own 'bone' and 'flesh'. After receiving her as such she is literally called "his woman." This was entirely a Divine institution operating as part of human nature and requiring no other authority than God's. (Genesis 2:25)

Let us pause to reflect on what all this reveals regarding the nature of the perfect man. While we acknowledge that some men are given the gift of singleness, most, like Adam, are not. Some religious people would have us believe that it is a sin to need a mate. This cannot be true, for the perfect Adam was created to have just such a need. In fact, without this "helper suited to him" he would have been unable to fulfill God's purpose for his life to "be fruitful and multiply...and rule." More than that he could not be God's glory— express God's character and headship authority—without her. As we have already seen, the cornerstone of Father God's character is a love that must be expressed. True to God's image within him, Adam too, needed to express the depths of his heart by being a source of love, protection, leadership, and the whole scope of spiritual, emotional, intellectual and physical depth created within him. Adam was not the stereotypical 'strong silent type,' out of touch with his emotions and unable to express himself. Look at how readily he was able to draw up his emotions and form them into a poem for his new love! What more could a woman want in a man?

The Dignity, Beauty And Capacity Of True Womanhood

That Adam loved and needed "his woman" there can be no doubt. She was a gift from God "suited to him." Notice the literal phrasing here. It is very specific. She was not just generally suitable, a generic woman—as if any of a number of feminine designs that God might have come up with would do. Not at all. She was "a helper suited to HIM." In every way she corresponded perfectly to his needs in a helper. You can be sure she had great spiritual, emotional, intellectual and physical capacities corresponding to his own. This would make for a satisfying and fulfilling relationship for them both. More than that, she could have the satisfaction of knowing that by applying all the great depth of her resources to being a "helper suited to" her husband she was fulfilling the dignified and valuable purpose for which God had created her. Adam was the head. She was his body. Together they were one. Together in this way they were the Lord's own image and glory ruling in the earth.

The Pattern For Real Marriage

Bear in mind that marriage means oneness. Eve had already received of Adam's life because of being created from his rib. On being received as one with him they were `married'. Of course, the man and woman were given the Divine mandate to "multiply," so they were free to express their oneness through sexual relations. The oneness of the first couple is duplicated in marriage after that original pattern through sexual relations. When a man gives a woman of his own life through intercourse he is making her `one flesh' with himself and is, in that sense, thereby married to her. Through this act he is obligating himself to her as her husband with all the responsibilities towards her that marriage entails. Sex is more - much more - than a mere physical act. Sexual relations create a physical, emotional and spiritual bond that continues to exert great effect on the inner spirit of men and women; long after the act itself is completed. (1 Corinthians 6:15-20)

The marriage of the first couple is God's pattern for real marriage. That pattern is repeated elsewhere in the Bible. (Genesis 24)

The pattern involves these essential elements:

1. God chooses the bride suited to His man.

2. The bride's head, usually her father (in this case, God) gives her to the man.

3. The bride and groom agree with God to marry as a lifelong commitment.

4. The marriage is consummated so that the woman becomes "one flesh" with her husband.

Anything beyond these elements is not essential to making a Godly marriage but is a concession to societal and cultural norms and needs. Family and society do have interests that normally need to be taken into consideration - although these are not essential to making a marriage. Counter-balancing that consideration is the fact that in some cases legal marriage may create obligations under the law of the state that go contrary to God's requirements and Will regarding true marriage. For this reason legal marriage and Biblical marriage are actually two entirely different relationships.

Marriage - A Word With Two Meanings

In such cases the parties involved may choose to forego 'legal' marriage while still being married before God. This is so because human marriage, which is a human contractual relationship, is not the same thing as Godly marriage. In fact, God is not even considered an essential party to a 'legal' marriage.

As an example of the fundamental difference between legal marriage and godly marriage consider this explanation of legal marriage. It refers to the State of Maine but is typical of most other localities: "There are really three partners to a marriage - the two persons who have decided that they want to be married and the State of Maine. The State gives its consent to a marriage by allowing a license to be issued once it is satisfied that doing so will violate none of its laws." [Do Your Own Divorce In Maine, Divorce Reform, Inc., 1982]

Godly marriage is also a relationship between three parties. In this case, though, the three parties are God, the man, and the woman. God specifically and Sovereignly brings together the parties of His choosing. In such a marriage the binding factor is the Will of God - not the sanction of human institutions. The man and woman bind themselves to that Will by becoming one flesh. As Y'shua said; "Give Caesar's things to Caesar and God's things to God." When did God ever give His authority over marriage to 'Caesar'? If He has not then godly marriage remains under the singular jurisdiction of heavenly authority.

With God basically missing from most people's lives society has had to find substitutes for His authority to 'marry' couples, that is, the organized church or the state. Generally, the Will of God has little, if anything, to do with such unions. The idea is that couples make their own choice as to whom they will marry and then God rubber-stamps the marriage when it is solemnized by the church or the state. Why God would lend His good Name to a union He never initiated is never contemplated. Is it any wonder that over half of such marriages today end in divorce? What more proof do we need that most unions produced within man's system are totally a product of human origin? Such simply are not marriages in the same sense as Godly marriages "made in heaven" where God brings the two together for His own glory.

That is not to say that two people, brought together by their own choice apart from God, cannot later choose to submit their lives and their union to Him. Where there is sincerity of heart and obedience to the sovereignty of God what is common can become sanctified, to His Glory. What is merely 'one flesh' can become 'one spirit' - with the touch of God. That is why believers should not abandon an unbelieving mate. By loyalty to the unbelieving mate God is glorified and the unbeliever may eventually be won over. On the other hand, if the union has no place in God's plan the unbeliever will eventually depart on his/her own. (1 Peter 3:1-3, 1 Corinthians 7:10-17)

God's Order Expressed In Marriage

Now let us examine the intended relationship of man and woman in marriage. What we have already seen is that the woman was viewed as part of the man's own body. As one cherishes his own body so a man should love and cherish his wife. This is fundamental. We have also seen that God created man first, in His own image; meaning reflecting the glory—the character and authority of God—on earth. We should also remember that God's intention in creating the woman for Adam was so that she could be "a helper suited to him." (Genesis 1:27, 2:7, 18)

Modern feminists may object to these facts. However, where humans disagree with God's Word it is they who need to change - not God. The Bible is clear and consistent, both in its statement of the facts and in its interpretation of them. I have merely repeated what the inspired Scripture already says: "A man...is the image and glory of God; but the woman is the glory of man, for man does not originate from woman, but woman from man; for indeed man was not created for woman's sake, but woman for the man's sake." (1 Corinthians 11:7-9 NAS)

The foregoing verses reveal a fundamental difference between the respective roles of men and women in God's Order. While men and women are equal in nature as humans they are not equal as to purpose and authority. As God's glory on earth, men are to express God's character and authority of Fatherhood - God's headship authority as noted above. Their focus needs to be on their Lord and their life and purpose should be in Him as their Head. The married woman, on the other hand, glorifies God in so far as she is a helper suited to her husband in carrying out his God-appointed mission. The man is her head and she fulfills her purpose, thus glorifying God, by submitting herself to her husband. She derives her life and purpose through him. (1 Timothy 2:9-15)

Apostolic Affirmation Of God's Order

Paul makes God's natural order of authority unmistakably clear; 'the head of every man is Messiah, and the head of the woman is the man, and the head of Messiah is God.' Note carefully that the divine order among men and women in creation is an expression and natural extension of the patriarchal order already existent in the relationship of God and His Son. Although equal as to nature with Father God Messiah, the Son, submits Himself willingly to the Father as His Head - deriving His purpose and sense of fulfillment from serving and submitting to His Father. This order then extends to man, who is to make pleasing Messiah, man's Head, his first concern. From there the woman is to follow Messiah's example and submit to her husband as her God-appointed head. In this God-ordained order the very image of God is expressed on earth to God's glory. (1 Corinthians 11:3 HNV, Philippians 2, John 1:1, Ephesians 5:22-33)

Notice again that real marriage is much more than just a relationship between two people. Three are involved—not two. The Lord has the highest authority in the marriage. He is to have the first place in the man's heart with the woman serving as his helper in his service of the Lord. This gives purpose and meaning to the relationship of the man and woman. By having his heart oriented first of all toward the Lord the man is able to receive the life and love of his Head as the supply he continually draws on to be a loving head to his wife. This order makes for a continual flow of life and love into the relationship of the man and woman, sustaining it over time. God's headship order thus provides for a constantly revitalized marriage. Some women crave the first place in their husband's heart—even ahead of the Lord. That is unwise. If the man succumbs and turns from the Lord to give his wife first place the marriage relationship will then collapse in on itself and eventually become spent.

Think Like Messiah

Sometimes marriage breaks down for imperfect humans in our failure to manifest God's love and humility. Headship is no excuse to be a tyrant, but rather a responsibility to love and nurture one's wife. Also, today the world believes that a woman's service to the interests of her husband and care for the family is demeaning. This sense of pride is contagious and can cause discontent with God's Order in marriage. What we all need is the attitude of Messiah, Who taught that it is service that makes one great and Who practiced that by serving to the point of death. Remember, God's Order reflects His nature and ways and is higher than the ways of fallen man.

God's Perfect Order Still Valid

The Divine order worked perfectly in Eden. Man was in constant fellowship with God. There was no such thing as sin. Adultery and divorce were not even thought of in the beginning. In perfection abuse of headship simply did not happen because the man loved his wife as his own body. Wifely submission must be a great deal easier when a woman is perfectly loved. Yes, it is all too true that we are no longer in paradise. Nevertheless, God has not revoked His perfect order in favor of something else for men and women on earth. We must look up to our heavenly Father to give us the grace we need that we might glorify Him by living as He intends. (Ephesians 5:22-33, Genesis 2:23-24)

From our standpoint we can barely imagine what the actual experience of daily life was like for the first human couple. We do know this much: God looked at all that He had created, with His crowning earthly achievement of man and woman completed, and He declared it "very good." Then He rested from His creative work. All was perfect. The man and woman were perfect. The order and pattern for a God-glorifying human society was now in place, and it too, was "very good." (Genesis 2:1-3)

You Are Very Good!

God considers humanity as he created it "very good." Think about that. God created the fullness of human capacities and abilities and considers all of that "very good!" How different is God's view from that of much of religion. Much of religion looks on various aspects of our humanity as intrinsically bad. Granted, much of what God created in man has been twisted into something evil. But let us not forget that humanity as God created it is "very good." That means our bodies and physical lives are very good. Our innate intelligence, talents and character used as God intended are very good. The expression and experience of the full range of human emotion and sensation under the control of the spirit within are very good. To need a mate as Adam needed the woman is very good. For a woman to derive her life from her husband as the first woman did is very good. To "be fruitful and multiply...and rule the earth" is very good! To fully express our humanity as God created and ordered it is challenging, joyous and glorifying to God. Seen this way, we must realize that expressing and growing into all of who and what we are meant to be as individual human beings is not only our God-given right - it is our joyous duty to our loving Creator.

Unchangeable Features Of God's Eternal Order

With God's rest from His creative work we have God's Order for the universe and for this earth established. Let us recap the fundamental principles of God's Order as we have found them in his Word:

1. The Creator is Sovereign over His creation. It is the obligation of every intelligent creature to obey God fully and unequivocally in all things by virtue of His Creatorship and Godship.

2. The primary motive of God's heart is love. It is grace that cannot be earned.

3. All authority is from Father God and is delegated through and for the Son, Who exercises the authority of God over all. This is according to the patriarchal nature of the First Family.

4. God, through His Son, individually created various forms and levels of spirit life and imbued each of them with power and authority suitable to their intended function and purpose.

5. God and His Son created man in their own image, to be God's glory in the earth. Man was created and equipped to live in perfect fellowship with God and in harmony with God's Order.

6. God created the earth and everything in it and gave dominion over all of it to man individually and secondarily to man and woman together. In this way the patriarchal authority of heaven was extended into the earth through man. Thus the Lordship of God would be expressed in human society through the lordship (small 'l') of man.

7. God made the woman from the man's own body to be one with him, to be his helper and his glory with the man as her loving head. The man, in turn, was to look to the headship of God. This is the substance of real marriage.

8. God gave the first couple the divine mandate "to multiply" and to "rule over the earth." Reproduction would be the means for the divinely bestowed authority to be passed on to each individual through the generations. This would make for individual freedom with the only authority over other humans being natural family authority in the image of God and His Son.

9. There are only two modes of existence as signified in the two trees; life in submission to God in harmony with His order or independence from God deciding for one's self what is right and wrong. The first way is life. The latter is death.

10. After putting all this into place God rested from His creative work and sanctioned it as being what He wanted by calling it "very good." It is a good thing to be human!

We could point out many more details, but these are the principle points pertaining to our discussion of God's established order. This is God's Order under the Reign of God.

Distinctiveness Within God's Creation

As we have seen, there is a great distinction between God's Order of life and authority for the spirit population as opposed to what God instituted in and for the family of man. Heavenly government includes hierarchical levels of authority as a structure of order among the individually created angels. This suits God's purpose in creating the Angelic life and is consistent with the nature of that life. Of course, it is the Personal involvement of God, through His Son and by His Spirit that imparts life to the heavenly order making it more than a dead bureaucracy.

God did not create man with anything like the angelic order of authority. The nature of man is different from that of the angelic life with a different purpose. As we have seen, man was made in the likeness of God and His Son. Humankind was created to reproduce with God-given authority to be passed on through reproduction. The kind of authority God gave man was in His likeness. It is the authority of Fatherhood. As the generations of mankind would increase in the earth that authority would become extended from fathers to grandfathers to great-grandfathers, etc. In other words, human society would naturally be organized according to a family and extended family (tribal) society. All authority would be exercised in love by those with some form of family authority. The control on this was the image of God in each human and the Personal guidance of God through Headship over each man. Willing and loving submission to God and God-given authority would result in a human society in perfect fellowship with God and in harmony with God's Order.

Freedom Inherent In God's Creation Of Man

God's Order would make for the greatest personal freedom for each individual, providing the framework within which each person could grow to be all that God put within them to be. Life would be filled with satisfying activity, love, joy, peace and plenty for each member of the human family. The joyous human family living in fellowship with God would reflect the multifaceted glory of the Heavenly Father! Only by submission to God within His established order can men and women glorify God as He created them to. If God's Order had continued to be expressed perfectly through the perfect race that Father God initiated, man would be forever free of the tyranny of bureaucratic and dictatorial government, not to mention war, crime, oppression and a whole host of societal and other ills. If all had followed the order of God there would never be anything like the slavery depicted in the shackle dream. Sadly, slavery rather than joyous freedom has become the lot of man.

Why Have We Strayed From Our Father's Love?

Please note, dear reader, that God gave us nothing but good. He is much more than our Creator. He is our loving Heavenly Father; fully deserving of obedient and loving children. Slavery and degradation were never a part of God's Order for man. They have no place in the Reign of God. God has not changed. God's Order has not changed nor has it ever been revoked. We are the ones who have changed. How did that happen? How could we have fallen so far?

Let us now give that question more than the usual superficial consideration.

4

REBELLION AND DISORDER

As the newlyweds enjoyed their idyllic honeymoon they were unaware that trouble was already starting to brew in paradise. It would come from a source that they, in their simplicity and innocence, had not yet come to know of.

Another Spirit

The only Spirit Person yet revealed to them was their Creator, with Whom they enjoyed blessed fellowship. As far as we know, even the Son had not yet been revealed in fullness. In the Father's wisdom He had reserved that revelation for a day still thousands of years in the future. There was another spirit in the garden, a high-ranking Cherub we call Lucifer (shining one, morning star) and perhaps others working under his authority. As a spirit, he was invisible to the human couple. This was by God's design to keep a separation between the heavenly and earthly order. There was no need for Lucifer to be known to the man and woman because he could perform his duty perfectly without their knowledge. His 'Boss' was God, not the man. He was a "Covering Cherub" with responsibility to "cover," or protect, the man and woman from any accidental harm that might come to them while exploring the many wonders of their garden home. "Covering" also included other duties of oversight of the Garden itself.

With the priority that God had given to this particular corner of the universe, to be assigned this duty was a great honor, indeed. We would expect that such an important task would be committed to one of God's most glorious creatures. The Scriptures indicate this was the case. Through the prophet Ezekiel God likens the Ancient King of Tyre to the covering cherub, and gives us a glimpse into unseen events in Eden:

"So says the Lord YHWH: You seal the measure, Full of wisdom and perfect in beauty. You have been in Eden the garden of God; Every precious stone was your covering...and the gold, the workmanship of your tabrets and of your pipes in you-in the day you were created, they were prepared. You were the anointed cherub that covers, and I had put you in the holy height of God, where you were." (Ezekiel 28:12-14 JPG)

The covering cherub of Eden was thus among the wisest, and most beautiful of God's angelic creatures. He was perfect as God created him. What then was the problem?

Ezekiel continues: "You were perfect in your ways from the day you were created, until iniquity was found in you...Your heart was lifted up because of your beauty; you corrupted your wisdom because of your splendor." (Ezekiel 28:15-17 JPG)

The prophet Isaiah, Likening the king of Babylon to this spirit, adds to our understanding: "O shining star (Lucifer KJV), son of the morning, how you have fallen from the heavens! You weakening the nations, you are cut down to the ground. For you have said in your heart, I will go up to the heavens; I will raise my throne above the stars of God, and I will sit in the mount of meeting, in the sides of the north. I will rise over the heights of the clouds; I will be compared to the Most High." (Isaiah 14:12-14 JPG)

The Corruption Of Lucifer

Putting the elements of God's revelation together we find that Lucifer was a perfect and glorious Cherub that was assigned the privilege and duty of covering in Eden. His heart became "lifted up because of (his) beauty." He allowed thoughts of his own beauty and importance to cause him to become prideful. This pride caused him to misuse his God-given wisdom to hatch a plot. In implementing his scheme he "corrupted his wisdom because of (his) splendor." Just what was the purpose of his scheme? God reveals Lucifer's objective; "I will go up to the heavens; I will raise my throne above the stars (angels) of God...I will be compared to the Most High." Lucifer was plotting the first rebellion. He would eventually "go up to the (spirit) heavens" with his malicious scheme to create a following there. He would actually compete with God for the throne![1].

Let us pause a moment to deal with the question that generally arises at this point. If Lucifer was perfect then how could he become prideful and sin? The answer is in the verses above. "Perfect" as used in the Bible means complete and blameless. Perfect does not mean unable to sin. God gave his intelligent creatures free will. That free will is part of the perfection with which they were created. At the same time, free will provides for a free choice to do something other than what God directs. That choice is always available to creatures with free will, perfect or otherwise. It was inevitable that some of God's intelligent creation would eventually make the alternative choice. Apparently, Lucifer became so filled with pride that he believed he should be the one to take advantage of the 'ground floor opportunity' and 'own the franchise' on rebellion. He would be the one to compete with God for the top spot in the universe.

The Object Of The Plot

How was this cunning spirit to make his grab for power? Remember, he could not create authority for himself. He could not create anything. He would have to twist God's creation and God's Order to usurp the authority that God had invested in others if his dream were to become a reality. Where was the logical place to start? Why, how fortuitous! Right where he was! God had invested dominion of the entire earth in Adam. All the generations to come along with all of their God—ordained authority were still in Adam's loins. If Lucifer could just "sign up" Adam in his rebellion he could get control of all that dominion of the earth, as well as potential headship authority of future generations. This was the mother of all pyramid schemes and it was just the launching point he needed!

Finding The Weakest Point

But now the question was, how would he get Adam to rebel? Look at all God had done for Adam. Look at the riches, both material and spiritual that Adam enjoyed from God's hand. Besides, being created in God's image, Adam had no inclination toward anything but loving obedience toward his loving Heavenly Father. There simply was no complaint against God that could be conceived of that Adam would be inclined to embrace. Obviously, a direct approach would never work. Only a very big lever would be able to pry Adam loose from God and onto Lucifer's side. It would have to be something that Adam was unprepared for—and something very close to Adam's heart. The lever that Lucifer would use could be none other than Adam's beloved wife. As a perfect helper, she was created with a nature of submission to another. It was natural for her to look to another person for direction. She had been equipped for her tender role of wife and mother with very sensitive and responsive emotions. Perhaps those feminine qualities could be perverted to Lucifer's advantage. Perhaps Lucifer could appeal to those more sensitive emotions and her natural responsiveness to get her to obey him rather than her husband! That's it! He would begin his grab for power by going after

Adam's beloved wife. To do so he would have to break her away from the protective headship of her husband.

We should say at this point that Adam's headship was not in the least tyrannical or dictatorial. It was a loving and nurturing sort of leadership. Having been created first, it was Adam's joyous duty to bring his wife up to speed on things. He must have enjoyed pointing out the different animals and teaching her the names that he had given them. As head, it fell to him to inform his wife about God and all he knew of God's Order. He must have told her about the Tree of Life and the Tree of Knowledge of Good and Evil. No doubt, he conveyed God's warning to not eat of the forbidden fruit. Sometimes they must have fellowshipped with God together in the Garden. However, Adam did not dominate her every moment. At times she chose to be alone, as healthy people sometimes do, and there is no record of Adam having any trouble with that. Adam respected her need for personal freedom.

Lucifer Makes His Move

It was at one of those times when Adam's wife was alone that Lucifer made his move. He either used some subtle means to lure her near the forbidden tree or waited for a time when she happened to be there. Lucifer kept his true identity concealed by speaking to the woman through a serpent, much like a ventriloquist speaks through a dummy. She was used to making marvelous new discoveries every day, so she had no reason to be suspicious of a talking serpent. Also, she would have no fear of the serpent because there was perfect peace between humankind and all the animal creation. Besides, she knew she had been given authority over the animals. The inspired record tells us about the encounter: "The serpent...said to the woman, Is it true that God has said, You shall not eat from any tree of the garden?"

And the woman said to the serpent, "We may eat of the fruit of the trees of the garden, but of the fruit of the tree which is in the middle of the garden, God has said, You shall not eat of it, nor shall you touch it, lest you die."

"And the serpent said to the woman, You shall not surely die, for God knows that in the day you eat of it, your eyes shall be opened, and you shall be as God, knowing good and evil." (Genesis 3:1-5 JPG)

Look carefully at these words. Lucifer did not speak according to the true motivations of his heart. He did not say "I'm plotting a rebellion against God because I want to steal God's Throne for myself. Do you want to join me?" She would certainly not have found the truth very appealing, so he kept his true agenda hidden. Instead, he began by asking her what seemed to be an innocuous question to get her thinking about the forbidden fruit. But what a question! "IS IT TRUE THAT GOD HAS SAID…" To even pose such a question is to suggest that God might lie! It was the first seed of doubt.

Lucifer Offers The Woman Liberation

When telling the serpent of God's command regarding the forbidden fruit it's interesting that "You shall not…touch it" was added to the original command. You can almost hear the echo of Adam's voice in this phrase, warning her to keep away from it. Her repetition of the command leaves no doubt that she was fully informed about the consequences of eating the fruit. Lucifer, like a "shining star" of liberation, tells her that she doesn't really have to worry about those consequences because God has lied to cover His hidden agenda! In other words, he was accusing God of doing what he, Lucifer, was himself doing at that very moment!

No, (went Lucifer's argument), God was not telling her to abstain from the fruit because he was concerned for her and did not want her to die. That's just what God wanted her to think. God was really trying to use fear of death to keep her from breaking free of His authority. Father God was manipulating her! Actually, if she ate the fruit she would find out that she would not die. More than that, she would actually be like God, knowing good and evil for herself. Only by choosing to disobey God could she become the wise, liberated woman she had the potential of becoming. Can you imagine that! God was depriving this poor, downtrodden woman of liberty by keeping her ignorant and in subjection. Obviously, her husband, who repeated the command to her, must either be in on the conspiracy to keep her down, or must be too ignorant to know the truth! … So went the logic of Lucifer's slanderous deception.

Lucifer's statement not only slandered God, but as we've observed, it also carried with it grave implications regarding the headship of Adam. Perhaps because of those implications the woman did not first consult with her husband and head before considering the voracity of Lucifer's claims. Instead, she thought about his words as she examined the fruit for herself. "And the woman saw that the tree was good for food, and that it was pleasant to the eyes, and the tree was desirable to make one wise. And she took of its fruit and ate; and she also gave to her husband with her, and he ate." (Genesis 3:6)

The Woman Was Deceived But Adam 'Wimped Out"

There can be no question that the woman fell for Lucifer's line. The apostle Paul confirms this, saying; "... Adam was formed first, then Eve. And Adam was not deceived, but the woman being deceived, has come to be in transgression." (1 Timothy 2:13-14)

Yes, the woman believed Lucifer's lie and, rejecting God and His Order, made a grab for the false `liberation' that the serpent was offering. The question remains; why did Adam disobey God, since he was not deceived? "..She also gave to her husband with her, and he ate." (Genesis 3:6)

When confronted by his wife, Adam went along with her in transgression. When faced with the choice, Adam abdicated his place of headship authority by putting his love for his wife before his loyalty to God. Adam has the larger blame here. He simply 'Wimped out' rather than displease his wife—and the whole human race would suffer because of it. Let this be a lesson to every man of God.

Lucifer's scheme had worked perfectly. He lured the woman with the promise of wisdom and liberation from submission to God and the headship of her husband. Thus Lucifer was able to bypass Adam's protective headship authority and get control of the woman through her more tender feminine emotional make-up. Once he had control over her he was able to use her to exert emotional pressure on the real object of the scheme - Adam. Thus the crafty serpent was able to pervert Adam's love for his wife into a lever pressuring him to obey Lucifer and so doing, to disobey God.

The Ruler Of The World!

This was a coup! He had succeeded in perverting God's Order to his own ends. God gave dominion to man. Man gave the authority to Lucifer by bowing to his control. Lucifer was now ruler of the world! In a single act of disobedience by our first father all mankind was sold into servitude to the unseen deceiver whose awful career as world tyrant Adam had just launched. Here is the answer to the question of how the unseen tyrant of the shackle dream first gained his position of power—man gave it to him! What that has meant for our suffering race is signified well by the slavery depicted in the shackle dream.

Of course, all that had not yet transpired when the woman, then the man, first transgressed. What would they do now that the deed had been done? Like naughty children or hardened criminals Adam and his wife thought they could hide their transgression and avoid the dire consequences. They would prove to be wrong about that—dead wrong.

FOOTNOTES:
    [1]. The 'Gap Theory' and Satan's fall. It has been widely held by some that an earlier world predating Adam had been created and that it was at the time of that earlier creation that Lucifer fell. Could this be true? Unger's Bible Handbook, Revised 1984 edition, page 30, comments on the 'Gap Theory': "'... Evangelical scholars have taken a variety of positions concerning the significance of the creation account in Gen 1:1-2:3. The opening words of Genesis have been commonly assumed to refer to the original creation of the universe. Some scholars prefer, however, to envision a relative beginning, allowing events such as Satan's fall and the geological ages of the earth to precede 1:1 or 1:2 (the Gap Theory).
The issue of a relative beginning (re-creation) principally revolves around three considerations:
    1.   Is the phrase, 'in the beginning,' absolute or relative?
    2.   Does the word 'create' (Heb. bara') possibly mean 'fashion or re-create'?
    3.   How do Gen 1:1 and 1:2 fit together grammatically and chronologically i.e., is it possible that a gap intervenes? The phrase, 'in the beginning', is construed by most Hebrew scholars as absolute. It should be noted though that the phrase, 'in the beginning' of John 1:1 antedates the 'in the beginning' of Gen 1:1 in any case.
The Hebrew term *bara'* has the basic meaning 'create' in distinction from the word *yasar* (to fashion, form). In most of its OT usages *bara'* speaks of 'creating something new' or 'bringing into existence' (Isa 41:20; 43:1; Ezk 21:30;28:13, 15). As a result, most exegetes argue that *bara'* serves as testimony to God's *ex nihilo* (out of nothing) creation. The phrase, 'Now the earth was formless and empty,' has been rendered, 'and the earth became...' to portray a chaotic visitation of divine judgment upon the original earth. To place a gap in 1:2 is untenable by the Hebrew text, which shows that all three clauses are circumstantial either to the main clause in 1:1 or that in 1:3."
    GENESIS, CREATION AND CREATIONISM, p. 123 by Lloyd R. Bailey, copyright 1993, adds this point: "What may one say about the proposed translation that allows the "gap theory" at Genesis 1:2 ("The earth BECAME without form...")? ...The Hebrew verb used there ordinarily means "to be," with the addition of a following preposition being necessary to give the meaning "to become." In fact,

in the KJV, every instance where this verb is translated "to become" involves the preposition, and the preposition is not found at Genesis 1:2. The major modern versions of the Bible in English (be they Jewish, Protestant, or Catholic; be they prepared by "conservatives" or by "liberals") do not render the verb here in any other sense than the familiar one from KJV: "And the earth WAS without form..." ...In short, it was only the need by some interpreters to find a time for an angelic rebellion and expulsion from heaven (based upon a misunderstanding of texts in Ezekiel 28 and Isaiah 14) that led to a forced and inaccurate translation ("became") at Genesis 1:2."

In addition to the evidence cited above showing the 'gap theory' and an accompanying fall of Satan at that time as being 'untenable' we have the further and even stronger testimony of the Scriptures themselves. At the end of all God's creative work at the end of the sixth creative day "God saw all that he had made, and it was very good. And there was evening, and there was morning -- the sixth day. Thus the heavens and the earth were completed in all their vast array." Gen. 1:31 NIV

If Lucifer and a third of God's heavenly host were already in a state of rebellion at that time it could not be said that all was "very good." Neither could it be said that the "heavens ... were completed in all there vast array" for the spiritual heavens would have been then existing in a decidedly incomplete, transitional situation. The picture painted at the end of the sixth day after the creation of perfect humankind is a picture of all things in heaven and on earth in perfect submission to the will of the Grand Creator - thus placing the rebellion of Lucifer as occurring at no other time than after the creation of man and woman. Thus the fall of 'the serpent' and the man and woman in the Garden as reported in the Genesis account was the original incident that marked the fall of all three - bringing rebellion for the first time into both heaven and earth, corrupting the perfect 'goodness' of the universe.

This timing is also treated as a given fact in Ezekiel 28:12-15, which portrays Lucifer as being 'perfect' as the 'covering cherub' ... 'in Eden, the garden of God.' Genesis 2:5-15 clearly shows that Eden was 'planted' by God in connection with the creation of man to be his home and was not a part of some earlier civilization. Thus Ezekiel adds his inspired testimony to the fact that Lucifer's rebellion must have occurred with the Rebellion in Eden as clearly reported in Genesis, and not at some speculative earlier date.

5

LIFE AND ANTI-LIFE

Life together in harmony with YHWH and His Order had been glorious, but now the honeymoon was over.

Living Outside The Loop

Adam and his wife had been allowed to eat freely of the Tree of Life because mankind was meant to live by the life of God and in perfect harmony with his organic order and life flow. Now he and his wife had eaten from the other tree, the Tree of the Knowledge of Good and Evil. So doing, they had chosen a life lived in independence from God and his ways according to their own knowledge of good and bad. That way of living—choosing for one's self what is good or bad—by definition cuts one off from God's personal guidance. That choice therefore alienates one from God's Order and from life itself as it flows from God. Granted, the deceiver's line sounds very tempting. It would seem that greater independence would mean greater freedom. However, independence from God, while seeming to offer freedom, actually subjects one to a life of slavery, vanity, pain and frustration because it moves against the flow of God's life and natural order. It ignores the Creator's will and purpose for all that he has created.

This is better understood when we realize that all the earthly creation - including the earth itself, the animal life, the plant life, and man and woman in God's Order of relationship to God, to each other and to the earth - all of that was created to be a complete organic system. After its completion God pronounced the whole of that complex system "very good." But what happens when some part of an organic system does not function as it should - or not at all? What happens when some part of an organic system mutates into some unintended form? Then the entire system is damaged, diseased and put at risk. Think about the effect of cancer or AIDS on the organic system of the human body and I think you'll get my drift. This is why independence from God could only result in death. Humans are just not smart enough to know what the far-reaching effects of their choices might be on themselves or the rest of the creation. Only God, Who created the entire organic system, has the wisdom to keep it all in proper balance. Only by relying on life from Him can we live life as it is meant to be within God's perfect order.

Sin Is Anti-life!

No wonder reliance on one's own judgment rather than on God is called "sin" in the Bible! Most people misunderstand the meaning of the term sin. They think of a sin as being theft, telling a lie, or some other violation of a code of right and wrong. While these things are sin, sin is much more than simply outward violations of a moral code. Sin is an impulse, a force within that moves us to please ourselves and to act according to our own standard of right and wrong rather than to simply live in the flow of the life of God. The word 'sin' has become loaded to the extent that I would like to coin a modern term to convey the real idea without the religious connotations that 'sin' has come to embody. Think of it as a law of the natural world, like the law of gravity, or inertia. I call this law, spoken of in scripture as the law of sin and death, "anti-life." (Romans 8:2)

The term fits. My dictionary [Webster's New World] offers this definition of the prefix anti: 1. Against; hostile to 2. that operates against 3. that prevents, cures, neutralizes 4. opposite; reverse 5. rivaling.

In the Garden the two trees stood for the only two modes of intelligent existence. Since the first is life the other opposing mode can be defined as anti-life with no harm to either the definition of the word or, what is more important, to the meaning of the Scriptures. As we have stated already, life is God's way. To choose life is to live in fellowship with God impelled by his Spirit of life as the moving force within—Spirit to spirit. This Life of the Spirit causes one to flow in perfect harmony with God's natural order. Presented as the opposite of the Tree of Life is the fruit of the Tree of the Knowledge of Good and Evil—anti-life. This is a seductive fruit indeed, calling the individual to reliance on one's own limited knowledge and understanding - a reliance on the lower resources of the soul. These include the impulses of the emotions fueled by the natural senses, and one's thoughts and reasonings—but leaving out the higher function of direct guidance from the Spirit through the spirit. This way is anti-life because everything about this way is rebellion against the true life of God, twisting and distorting the order of God and causing pain, disease, moral and physical corruption, and death.

Anti-life Is The Degenerative Force In Man

People think they are living life. Most are not. They are living anti-life. It is the inheritance of every descendant of Adam and Eve. Like some loathsome disease with which our first parents infected themselves [and their realm], they could do nothing else but pass on what they had to us. Anti-life is the force at work within all of us undermining everything good that God has put within us. Anti-life is ever seeking to tear down the image of God within, to minimize us, diminish us, and destroy us - all in the name of a dubious independence and freedom. Who lives that has not experienced this destructive force within that, like a hungry spreading cancer, is part of our own organism? This is anti-life and there is no medicine you can take, there is no philosophy you can adopt, there is no surgery that can be had that can remove this scourge from your organism and your being. There is only one antidote, only one remedy for its awful effects. Anti-life must be overcome and swallowed up by an onrushing flow of the powerful life of God!

Effects Of Anti-life On The First Couple

But enough of that for now, lest we get too far ahead of ourselves. The point here is the effect of the anti-life fruit on our first parents. God said that in the day they ate from the fruit they would surely die. That's exactly what happened. They ceased living Life—that's death. Their spirits were dead. They were dead as to fellowship with God. They were dead as to their future in paradise. They were dead as to growing into all they could have become in God's plan. They were dead as to fulfilling their reason for being—to glorify God. That their bodies took a while to manifest that death by actually returning to the dust was quite irrelevant from God's standpoint. Death of the body would also surely come as the final blow of the anti-life existence they had chosen.

Guilt And Shame

Immediately upon eating of the fruit life was over and anti-life began. Notice its manifestations: "And the eyes of both of them were opened, and they knew that they were naked. And they sewed leaves of the fig-tree, and made girdles for themselves." (Genesis 2:7 JPG)

All of a sudden they decided their nakedness was evil. They weren't feeling very good about themselves, were they? Two basic characteristics of anti-life, guilt and shame, had set in.

Fear And Hiding From God

"And they heard the sound of YHWH God walking up and down in the garden at the breeze of the day. And the man and his wife hid themselves from the face of YHWH God in the middle of the trees of the garden. And YHWH God called to the man and said to him, Where are you? And he said, I have heard your sound in the garden, and I was afraid, for I am naked, and I hid myself." (Genesis 2:8-10 JPG)

The tragedy of these verses is beyond words. Oh, the loss! The terrible, terrible, loss! The precious fellowship that Adam had enjoyed with His loving Creator Whom he had daily walked with and talked with and knew on 'a first Name basis'—was now replaced by fear and an inclination to hide from God. God calls and the answer is "I'm naked, I have something wrong with me, I'm not good enough, God won't accept me, I'm afraid—so I must hide from God." This is the voice of separation from God. This is the voice of anti-life. Now it was the voice of a guilty and fearful Adam.

Here is another hallmark of anti-life—unhealthy fear. Unhealthy fear of God. Fear of death. Fear of pain. Fear of loss. Living in God's life and love there is and has never been any unhealthy fear. With anti-life, fear is one of the principal motivators. Before our eyes we are seeing the shackles and chains of the shackle dream take shape. First doubting God, then selfishness, then independence from God, then outright rebellion, then guilt, shame, inadequacy and fear form the neck shackle and some major links of the chain by which Lucifer binds men and women to his framework of slavery. Each of these anti-life characteristics is a button wired directly into the heart - a button that the deceiver can push at will from his invisible position of power to control his ignorant and pathetic underlings.

Passing Blame

I hope you don't think we've named all the anti-life buttons, links in the chain of slavery, the characteristics of the anti-life sin nature. Adam and his wayward wife reveal some more in their reluctant encounter with God.

"[God] said, Who told you that you were naked? Have you eaten of the tree of which I commanded you not to eat"?

They foolishly thought they could hide from this, the day of reckoning. Anti-life always seems to think that. But that day always comes eventually. When it does what is the response of anti-life? Genuine sorrow for violating God and His order? Perhaps a real, heartfelt accepting of the responsibility for one's wrong actions followed by a willingness to do whatever is needed to correct the situation? How about a humble request for forgiveness and restoration? Not a chance! The response of anti-life is to deny responsibility by blaming someone else! True to the sin nature, Adam blamed his wife - and, get this, God - for giving her to him. The woman was not about to accept that. She passed the buck to the serpent. (Genesis 3:12,13)

They Were Ruined!

Who was really accountable? They all were, of course. Free will is a great thing when we make the right choice, but it also means we are responsible for wrong choices. A wrong choice is anything we choose that is contrary to God, His life, His ways, His order and His word to us. Wrong choices always have an impact on God's plan for us and on the lives of others. Adam, the woman and the deceiving spirit behind the serpent had all made wrong choices. Some would say that they just made a mistake and a loving God should overlook it and just let it go by. But on what basis? None of the three had accepted any responsibility or shown any remorse. Sure, they hid so they would not be punished, but that is an entirely different thing than real repentance. They gave no reason to believe they wanted to be restored to the perfection of character they had previously enjoyed. There was no reason to believe that if perfection were restored to them as a gift they would not simply choose sin again. They were ruined.

Judgment Follows Sin

God had warned them this would happen if they disobeyed Him. He told them they would die. Now it was time for God to follow through and pronounce judgment on them—to tell them what the specific effects of sin would be, to enforce His Word, and to protect His established order and purpose.

Appropriately, God began by pronouncing sentence on the unseen deceiver behind the serpent. Since our focus at this point is the effect of anti-life on the first couple we will come back to pick up this vital thread regarding the serpent shortly. The anti-life shackle links that we've noted so far seem to apply equally to all, whether male or female. However, man and woman were created with some major differences. It is to be expected that anti-life would have some dire effects unique to each gender. God's judgment of the man and woman separately confirms and illuminates that observation. Let's see what the unique anti-life effects would be on man and woman as we examine God's righteous judgment.

6

HOW SIN CORRUPTS
EACH GENDER

The man and woman had perverted God's Order and His judgment of them centers on the dire effects that would result to them as a result of that perversion. Because they were each created for different purposes with different capacities sin would have certain unique effects on each gender. Consider first God's judgment on Woman.

God's Judgment On Woman

He said to the woman, I will greatly increase your sorrow and your conception; you shall bear sons in sorrow, and your desire shall be toward your husband and he shall rule over you." (Genesis 3:16 JPG)

The woman had believed the deceiver's promise of wisdom and with it liberation from the headship authority of God and her husband, so she was deceived into choosing that path. Where did it lead womankind? Not to enlightenment and freedom - Increased womanly sorrows would be the result of feminine independence; unbridled by the protection that submission to the husbandly headship of God's Order would have otherwise offered. Now her lot would be increased "sorrow" and "conception."

Increased Sorrow And Conception

As an illustration of the relationship between increased conception and diminished headship consider the huge social problem of unwanted teenage pregnancies in America right now. Over the last 30 years the headship of fathers in America has been all but completely undermined by the feminist revolution. Before that happened fathers exercised a great deal more protective authority over their teenage daughters and the incidence of pregnancy out of wedlock was drastically less than it is now that girls are brought up to be 'liberated'. Back then, in most of the relatively rare cases when an unmarried girl did get pregnant the responsible party would accept the responsibility of becoming her husband. Without the degree of fatherly headship and order that existed just a generation ago the problem of increased conception among teenage girls has become so great, that as of this writing, it is widely believed that even the United States government can't afford to pay for all the babies!

Some versions render the phrase as "increased pain in childbirth." While this is generally included in the scope of the verse it is not the literal meaning of the phrase. This aspect and the whole woeful array of reproductive problems and motherly sorrows would come under the continuing phrase "You shall bear sons in sorrow." When God says "I will increase...conception" He means just that. The literal meaning of the verse; that God would increase conception now that the woman was in transgression, is the intended meaning. The rest of the verse sheds light on why God would do so.

Is Male Headship A Result Of The Fall?

This brings us to the most controversial part of the verse; "your desire shall be toward your husband and he shall rule over you." Some say that by this verse God instituted husbandly headship as a punishment for the woman's deception into sin. If that was so then headship was not part of God's perfect order but came in only as an adaptation to conditions related to the fall. Anyone who teaches this is either ignorant of the clear scriptural statement on headship written by the apostle Paul; or they refuse to accept God's Word spoken through the Lord's inspired apostle. In either case, such persons are not to be believed. 1 Corinthians 11, which we considered in an earlier chapter, provides the definitive statement of God's Word showing that headship is a part of God's natural order originating in God and passed on to man and woman at their creation in the perfect state. Not only that, but as we have seen, the details of the Genesis account are in perfect agreement with Paul. That being the case, what does Genesis 3:16 actually mean?

The Tendency Toward Female Control

This is not a matter of speculation because the Scriptures themselves make the meaning clear. Only fifteen verses later, in Gen. 4:7, the same Hebrew construction is used as in the verse under consideration. Therefore, to understand one is to understand both. This is more than a fortuitous accident. This second use of the same construction is obviously intended by the author to pick up the thread of the earlier verse. In Genesis 4:6-7 God is warning Cain that sin was seeking to get control over him and that Cain needed to take proper authority over it: "YHWH said to Cain, Why have you angrily glowed, and why has your face fallen? If you do well, is there not exaltation? And if you do not do well, sin is crouching at the door; and its desire is toward you; but you should rule over it."

The meaning of this verse is very clear: sin's "desire was toward" Cain in the sense of seeking to control him and he was being warned to "rule over it" rather than to allow himself to be controlled by sin.

Now let's compare the two verses: God's words to Cain: "[sin's] desire is toward you; but you should rule over it." (Genesis 4:7)

God To the woman: "your desire shall be toward your husband; and he shall rule over you." (Genesis 3:16)

Notice that the two verses are essentially the same, with the same meaning. At this point the meaning should be quite clear: The woman would seek to control her husband and he should properly resist that control by ruling over her in a proper Biblical sense. This meaning fits flawlessly in context as the next verse carries forward this theme, severely castigating Adam for failing to rule over the controlling influence of his wife. (Genesis 3:17)

Eve Had Initiated The Battle Of The Sexes!

With this verse God informs the woman on how sin would be manifested in her relationship with her husband. She would seek to control him and he would respond by struggling against that control. With God removed from first place in the marriage the perfect order that God had intended had given way and the relationship of the man and woman would collapse in on itself. The woman would no longer be content with her place as a "helper suited to her husband" with the purpose of glorifying God as the higher motive for her subjection. Now, with the selfish anti-life at work in her being, she would develop her own agenda according to the longings of her now-perverted feminine emotions. She would seek to achieve her ends through using her emotions to manipulate and control her husband. If he was to maintain any glimmer of the headship glory of God left within him he would resist that control and exert his authority. He would have to do this to maintain his manhood.

The battle of the sexes had been set up by the woman's rejection of her husband's rightful headship. That battle has raged with ever-increasing fury down to this day. This is the greatest curse of life for men, who, also plagued by the anti-life nature, often respond wrongly to feminine control tactics. Those wrong responses range from brutal domination on one end of the spectrum to total emasculation on the other. Abandonment of God's Order of loving headship and willing submission would mean greatly increased sorrow for both men and woman.

Why Increased Childbirth?

This brings us back to the first part of the verse and the reason God would respond to the woman's sin by an increase of childbirth. The apostle Paul seems to have this very verse in mind when he writes: "Let a woman learn in silence, in all subjection. But I do not allow a woman to teach, nor to exercise authority over a man, but to be in silence [in so far as teaching men or having authority over a man is concerned]. For Adam was formed first, then Eve. And Adam was not deceived, but the woman being deceived has come to be in transgression [through rebellion against her role as man's helper]; but she will be delivered through the bearing of children, if they [women] remain in faith and love and holiness, with sensibleness." (1 Timothy 2:11-15, brackets mine to explain meaning in context. Genesis 3:16)

This statement of Paul is not meant to be demeaning to woman. Its purpose is to promote a respect for and adherence to God's Order among God's people. It reveals a matter-of-fact understanding that the fallen inclination of women is to control men and it sets out the Godly response for God's men - not to allow it. It also ties back to God's increasing childbirth; explaining increased childbirth as a way of delivering women from involving themselves in controlling men. By expending their feminine resources on caring for their children they would be guarded from the sinful tendency to seek authority over men—which tendency they inherited from the first woman.

A Word To Modern Women Of God

While this book is being written primarily for God's men, I know some women will read it also. Ladies, if you are still reading this, God love you! I know this is hard to receive. Especially in this age when God's Order is spurned and/or simply unknown. But keep in mind that we are considering sin and its results. More than that, we are considering God's judgment of the woman's transgression. We should not expect this to be very complimentary. Paul is not attacking you and neither am I. All of this is being presented because we must know the truth to deal with it. If control coupled with an insubordinate attitude is a dominate trait of the fallen feminine sin nature let's admit it and deal with it. Denial will do nothing to alleviate the problem. As I write this I am confident that there are Godly women out there whose foremost desire is to glorify God. I know such women will make use of this truth for exactly that purpose.

Womanhood Itself Perverted By Sin

As we look back on all the implications of God's judgment of the woman it is, admittedly, almost too much to stand. It seems that every noble characteristic of womanhood had been subverted by the anti-life fruit. We notice that God's judgment on the woman is more than a generic judgment against sin in general. It is far more personal than that. It goes right to the center of who she is. It penetrates to the very core of her womanhood.

God's Judgment On Man

Now we turn our attention to God's judgment on the man. God begins by telling the man why he is being judged: "Because you have listened to the voice of your wife, and have eaten of the tree about which I commanded you, saying, you shall not eat from it..." (Genesis 3:17)

Man Had Put Woman Above God

God's point is crystal clear. Adam had obeyed the voice of his wife rather than the command of God. By this act, Adam had literally turned God's headship order upside down. As we have already read, God's Order calls for the Lord to be man's head and man to be the woman's head. What Adam did was therefore a terminal breach of trust with his Head whom he had disregarded in favor of entering into sin with his wife. It also amounted to an abdication of the rulership and headship authority that God had invested in him. This was the sin of Adam and the same sin would plague men for ages to come.

God's Man Must Resist Feminine Control!

The man of God is to be God's glory in the earth. He insults God and God's Order, not to mention his own manhood, when he allows himself to be manipulated by feminine control. The examples of those who have failed at this are as numerous as sons of Adam born on earth. God warns against it continually throughout His written Word.

Here are two examples:

"With persuasive words, she led him astray. With the flattering of her lips, she seduced him. He followed her immediately, as an ox goes to the slaughter, as a fool stepping into a noose. Until an arrow strikes through his liver, as a bird hurries to the snare, and doesn't know that it will cost his life." (Proverbs 7:21-23)

"Don't give your strength to women, nor your ways to that which destroys kings." (Proverbs 31:3)

The True Measure Of Manhood

Some feel that what makes a real man is being a good husband and father. God knows, we need more good husbands and fathers. But it would be a mistake to think that this alone is the true essence of manhood. The part of man that is directed toward other humans is but one side of the coin of the creature called man. The other side of the coin is the source of true manhood. I am talking about the side of man that is directed toward God. For let us not forget that even as woman was made to be man's glory—so also was man made to be God's glory. What real manhood is all about is that passionate and intimate bond between the individual man and his Heavenly Father. Real manhood means sonship—it means expressing the glory of the Father.

To be a true man is to be a true son of the Father. The true son lives in the life of the Father. He longs to be close to Him, to learn from Him, to be like Him, to please Him. The true son lives from and for his Father. The essence of real manhood is in the fierce passion for God around which the whole being of God's man is formed. This special relationship between God and His man is a sacred thing; an individual, personal and intimate thing. It must be hallowed ground upon which no one else may be allowed to intrude—not even a man's own wife. I do not mean by this that a man should not share in worship with his wife or teach his wife about God. I simply mean that at the core of true manhood is the Father-son connection that transcends all other relationships. You must be a man to really understand what this is about—and not just any man—you must be God's man—you must be God's son.

Sonship Is The Source Of True Manhood!

Being a good husband and father was meant to be the result of first being a good son. As a son is loved and guided by his Father he learns how to love and guide his wife and family. As the man draws on the life and love of his Father he receives his supply from which his wife and family might draw from him. This is God's way for man. It was so in the beginning and it is still so. By this I do not mean to imply that wives and children do not need their own personal relationship with God, for clearly, they do. What I am pointing out is that the root of real manhood is not to be found in man's relationship to woman—but rather, to God. Oh, that God's men today might come to understand this! But alas, most are still mired down in the sin of Adam, so preoccupied with pleasing the women in their lives that they fail to be real men, putting God FIRST! Such men have been "civilized" to the point of being shamefully emasculated.

From Ruler To Slave

Adam was God's son and thus lord of the world. His authority derived from his sonship. Because he esteemed his wife above God he failed in his loyalty as a son. He forfeited the fullness of manhood and he lost his noble authority over the earth. He would now be reduced to the sorrowful life of a toiling slave. God said, "The ground shall be cursed because of you; you shall eat of it in sorrow all the days of your life. And it shall bring forth thorns and thistles for you, and you shall eat the plant of the field. By the sweat of your face you shall eat bread until your return to the ground. For you have been taken out of it; for you are dust, and to dust you shall return."

The Creation Cursed Because Of Man

As lord of the earth man's deviation from the reign of God would have devastating effects on man's realm. The earth was brought under a curse that has affected every living thing in man's domain. All of nature was pushed out of balance, "cursed," by man's choice to abandon God. Man's lordship over the earth seems to have been turned upside down by his disobedience. Now the earth would be his master. He would live a life of toil eking out an existence from it until the enormous forces of the natural world would literally wear him out. Finally, his vanity would be complete when he would be absorbed back into the earth as mere dust. He had broken the vital pipeline of life and authority from God. Now he would find that in himself he had nothing to replace it with. True manhood had given way to vanity, toil and death.

Men: Don't Wimp Out!

What better illustrates the folly of putting one's wife and family ahead of God than this? If Adam had refused to follow his wife into transgression it appears that he would have had to endure the loss of his beloved wife because her sin would have its consequences. However, despite that loss, If Adam had remained obedient to his Father in the face of his wife's disobedience he would have retained a blessed inheritance to share with his offspring. A paradise home, a perfect and joyful life in fellowship with God and eternal life itself would have flowed through Adam to all of his children—born through a new woman, if needed. I say 'if needed' because according to God's principles of headship a pledge entered into by a wife is not binding if not validated by her husband. This suggests that if Adam had not accepted the fruit his deceived wife may have been corrected, repented and then been restored. (Numbers 30:10-12)

Men of God, the point is this: When a man puts God first he is doing what's best for his family, too. Unfortunately, Adam caved in to his wife and lost his fortune. The paradise home, the joyful life, the fellowship with God, eternal life—all were lost. Adam passed little more on to us than sin, toil, corruption and death—all because he cared more for his wife than for his Father.

The Pain Of Futility

Still, something of God's image continued to show through this fatally flawed vessel of earth. The image of God's character, capacities and nature had been built into this prototype man. Now in

n fell short of God's glory, though something of God's glory
ꞌinsic to the human creation. This has been the real pain
ꞌmanity: to be caught in between the full expression of
ꞇory and the blissful ignorance of mere animals. In ourselves
ꞇre aware enough to know we don't measure up while also lacking
ꞇhe perfection to do so. This is futility—vanity. It is only because we
retain something of God's image that some of us can see the futility
to which our race, even the whole of creation, has been subjected.

This futility, and the sorrow it causes, is so evident in the fallen
nature of both men and women respectively. Being cut off from their
Father the world's men lack the source of love and good order they
need to function as men. They are out of touch with sonship. True
manhood eludes them as they struggle for identity. Male sexuality
becomes fallen and twisted. Male authority becomes tyrannical or
cowers before inadequacy. Men look to women for validation as men
rather than to God. Thus, women become objects for the use of men or
are empowered to control men—or both. What we see from any angle
is that true manhood has been undermined to its very foundations
by sin. With the foundation eroded only a faltering shell remains,
still revealing the vaguest image of the glorious manhood that could
have been. Without real men as fathers and husbands, women are
denied the fullness of love and authority they need to flower into all
they could become. Self-protection and a controlling spirit seek to
compensate for rejection and lack of real love. Womanhood itself is
undermined and pain is felt throughout.

Sonship Holds Out Hope!

Yes, Manhood, Womanhood and all creation were frustrated
and subjected to futility by God's judgment against the rebellion
of our first human parents. This is a dismal picture. Let us face the
reality, but let us also conclude our examination of this tragedy with
a word of hope. For even while Father God allowed the rebellion to
take place he had already envisioned the plan by which liberation
would come. He kept that plan as a hidden treasure in His heart as
the one hope of creation. As the Great Patriarch, He would set things
right according to His own order—through sonship: "The creation
waits in eager expectation for the sons of God to be revealed. For the
creation was subjected to frustration, not by its own choice, but by
the will of the one [God] who subjected it, in hope that the creation

itself will be liberated from its bondage to decay and brought into glorious freedom of the children of God." (Romans 8:19-21)

Let us now see how God gives the first clue regarding this hope as we go back to examine His judgment against the serpent.

the

7

THE GREAT FAMILY FEUD

Deceit Through Stealth

It would appear that Lucifer's plot had succeeded. He had managed to pervert God's Order to acquire man's lordship over the earth for himself. His ruse of using the serpent, and his manipulation of the innocent, receptive wife of Adam worked out just as he had envisioned. Perhaps he felt that he had proved himself to be God's equal in wisdom. In truth, what he had displayed was not wisdom. It was merely opportunistic deceit.

Of course, what made the plot work was that the man and woman knew nothing about the devious spirit that had been behind the serpent's words. Even now that they had forfeited all, they continued in ignorance of how and why it had really happened—of who was really behind their fall from perfection. All that is reported in the Genesis account is what they actually knew about the encounter at the time—all they had seen was the serpent. Therefore, the account speaks from their perspective, with God's judgment falling upon the serpent. God did not find it appropriate to 'bring them up to speed' on the real identity of the serpent. That would be revealed, as we have seen, at a much later date.

God's Judgment On The Serpent

However it appeared to the man and woman, God's words were in reality directed beyond the dumb serpent to the treacherous betrayer who had hidden behind it: "And YHWH God said to the serpent, because you have done this, you are cursed above all beasts, and above every animal of the field. You shall go on your belly, and you shall eat dust all the days of your life. And I will put enmity between you and the woman, and between your seed and her seed—He will bruise your head and you shall bruise His heel." (Genesis 3:14-15 JPG)

Lucifer had chosen the serpent to be his 'mascot' and he would be forever identified with the serpent. Through God's judgment on the serpent He revealed what the end would be for Lucifer. It appears that the serpent was exceptionally intelligent and beautiful within the animal kingdom, probably with legs enabling it to stand upright. In cursing the serpent God took its legs out from under it, removing it from its position of honor and power. Now it would have to slither on its belly in the dust, with nothing but cunning to capture its prey.

Now every time a man of God would see a serpent in the dust he would be reminded of God's judgment on the Deceiver.

The Perfection Of God's Judgment

God's judgment of the serpent revealed a perfect understanding of Lucifer and his deceit. The unseen spirit would still have us believe his lies. He would have us believe that our loving Father only wants to dominate us through fear. He would have us believe that we can live forever and be "like God" ourselves—independent from our Creator. He would have us believe that we can ignore God's headship order and that in ignoring it we will have freedom. But God's judgment on the serpent reveals the truth: all of this is 'smoke and mirrors'—a crafty illusion that the deceitful snake uses to catch his prey. Watch out! The prey he is seeking is YOU!

Lucifer was once exalted with honor and authority in heaven. Like the serpent, he too, has had his legs taken out from under him. His realm would now be 'the dust of the earth' where he has established his power base through deceit with the delegated authority God had given to man. He was Lucifer no more. Now he would be called what he was—devil and satan. For devil means 'slanderer,' 'false accuser.' Satan means 'Adversary.' A good name—since he has made himself God and man's first and greatest enemy.

God's Authority - Even In Satan - Must Be Respected!

God's judgment of the serpent assumes God's recognition of satan's authority over his newly acquired earthly domain. God had given rulership of the earth to man and man gave that rulership over to satan. Therefore, the authority of satan is genuine, having originated in God. Since all authority is from God He would honor that authority that had been passed to the enemy. God is One—He must be true to Himself and His own ways.

In heaven this matter of authority from God is much better understood than it is on earth. Thus, "... even the archangel Michael, when he was disputing with the devil about the body of Moses, did not dare to bring a slanderous accusation against him, but said, "The Lord rebuke you!" (Jude 1:9)

The faithful archangel Michael would not offend God's authority in satan, but in respect for God "did not dare" to accuse him.

Oh, that God's earthly servants might learn such respect for God's awesome authority! If only we would learn to honor all authority originating in God then satan would be denied a vital weapon in his arsenal of destruction and deceit. It is not a matter of whether we happen to like the person or entity wielding the authority. It is not a matter of whether the authority is properly used or abused. All that matters is whether the authority originates in God. If it does it must be respected if we would honor our Father. Let us remember that even the Son of God, when on earth, acknowledged the rulership authority of satan, calling him "the ruler of this world" on several occasions. (John 12:31, 14:30, 16:11)

Satan's Serpentine Character And A Brood Of Vipers!

While satan's rulership authority ultimately originates in God, his proud and greedy character insured that he would venture well beyond the bounds of that authority. God's serpent metaphor looks into the future to reveal satan's hidden motives and ways. He would be a sleazy politician, able to seduce many over onto his side through his deceitful deal-making and outright lies. These others God refers to as satan's 'seed'. Having a 'seed' he would be a father of sorts. How ironic that even Satan must work within the patriarchal order that God has woven into the very fabric of the universe! Only, like everything he touches, he would twist and pervert it to his own evil ends. He was a father already—the father of lies. Through lies he would raise up offspring. In talking to some of them thousands of years later Messiah confirms this: "You belong to your father, the devil, and you want to carry out your father's desire. He was a murderer from the beginning, not holding to the truth, for there is no truth in him. When he lies, he speaks his native language, for he is a liar and the father of lies." (John 8:44)

Enmity Between Two Camps

Satan was given a free hand to raise up an evil seed. However, he and his seed would not go unopposed. There would be a struggle, a tension, hatred, 'enmity' between satan and his seed on one side and 'the woman' and her seed on the other side. This is strange language. Normally it is the father who is spoken of as providing the seed. This must have left satan feeling quite uneasy. Who was the 'woman?' Was it the woman before him that he had already so easily defeated through his deceit? Was it womankind? Was it some special woman God had in mind? Whatever woman it was, she would produce a seed that would be merely bruised by satan. That seed would then deliver a deathblow to satan's head! Satan, and all the population of heaven for that matter, must have wondered just what woman and what seed YHWH was talking about. One other question: There could be no seed without a father—so who was the father? The answers were to remain a mystery for thousands of years. The answers were in God's mind and He was not ready to reveal them.

Might Makes Right Is Not God's Way

One thing was clear though. satan had challenged God's authority and righteousness. If anyone expected to see this rebellion met by lightning bolts obliterating the rebels it wasn't happening. Clearly, the Almighty had the power to destroy these rebels and start over. However, God was not choosing to win through the principle of "might makes right." That is a principle of satan—not God. Rather, His judgments acknowledged the reality of the rebellion that had been brought into the world. He would let it run its natural course. God was willing to wait for the truth actually played out in human experience to bear Him out. This was in perfect harmony with His nature as the God of Truth.

This great drama is even now being acted out on the stage of the universe. Therefore, do not ask 'why' when you see trouble, pain, misery and death. Much less should you join the devil in accusing God of unrighteousness in allowing sin to have its consequences. God is righteous. There is no one to blame for suffering but satan and his seed.

God Is Not To Blame For Wickedness And Sorrow

But the accusation goes further: "If God is all knowing then He knew the rebellion was brewing even before it happened. He could have stopped it then and saved the human race from ever experiencing all the pain of sin and death. Since He could have stopped it but didn't that makes Him responsible." This accusation is at best a half-truth and an over-simplification.

Of course Father God knew what was going to happen. That did not obligate Him to interfere with the choice of beings whom He had created with the capacity of free choice. Besides, in a universe of intelligent creatures with free moral choice this issue of submission to God vs. independence was a real issue that inevitably had to be addressed. Freedom of thought insured that it would come up eventually. Since it is not in God's nature to suppress the truth He would allow the issue to be raised and eventually settled in the sight of all. There is nothing evil in that. It is, rather, the wisdom of a Father looking after the long-term interests of His family. This is especially so, since through the fall and His response to it He would reveal both Himself and His sons to all creation. Through this revelation the creation would not only be restored to its former glory—it would be elevated to a higher level of glory—even the glorious freedom of the sons of God! (Romans 8:21)

Life And Growth Reveal The Truth

As we observe God's ways we get to know Him. The Father's way of dealing with the rebellion is according to the principle of life and growth. Father God works through life and growth and the manifestation of the truth that emerges from that process. That's in His nature. In this case God indicated that two families would grow up into the world to struggle through to the conclusion of satan's challenge. One family would include the woman and her seed. The other would include satan and his seed. Like plants of the earth, both families would be allowed to grow up into their full growth, expressing the fullness of the character of the life in them. It would be a long and painful process. In the end right would prevail and satan would be crushed. Only then could all the terrible damage brought into the world through rebellion and perversion of God's Order be corrected.

Here's The Big Picture

Back then Father God gave no definition to the identity of the respective members of the two families beyond what was already known. He would allow the outworking of events and corresponding revelation to unfold the answers for all to see. Now, thousands of years since the beginning of the rebellion, we have most of the answers with a small but vital part yet to be revealed. Here is the broad picture that has emerged:

The woman is God's woman, His corporate wife, whom He patiently raised up and cultivated over the centuries. In course of time she grew into a woman, the woman, Israel. Because she is of the earth she has had a hard time learning her Husband's ways. Often she has been self-willed and wayward. Nevertheless, He has loved her, He has taught her, He has corrected her and countless times He has forgiven her and washed her clean. In all of this He has revealed the depth of His own nature to the universe. Regardless of her faults and failures it is not for the children to judge their mother. Rather, it is their duty to honor her. If we would know the ways of our Father's household we must not neglect the knowledge and ways of our mother. For she has been carefully schooled and cultivated, fitted to the Father's own ways over centuries of time. That's something that deserves to be respected.

Though His woman is of the earth the Father is of heaven. The Life He put within her as the loving bond of union was the Life of Divine Seed, His Own Beloved Son. That Seed of God and His woman was "bruised in the heal" by the enemy - to the point of death on the cross. "Bruised in the heal" because death could not hold Him! He is the Victor, through His own death conquering satan and all of his works! The final crushing of satan is yet future. That crushing will occur under the feet of the corporate Seed - The Son and the sons of God to be revealed. Take heart, sons of God; "The God of peace will soon crush satan under your feet." Just what all of this means for us at this point in the unfolding of our Father's plan is what this and following volumes are all about. (Romans 16:20)

Satan's Woman

Satan raised up a corporate woman also. In keeping with his character she is also a manipulator and a deceiver. She prides herself on her modern, independent thinking. She is not a wife—she would not dream of committing her affections to one husband—not unless it was a deceit to get something she wanted. She is a shameless whore who uses the allurements of the flesh for power and control—and to enrich herself. She is known by different names. The most infamous is found in Revelation 17:5: "This title was written on her forehead:

MYSTERY BABYLON THE GREAT THE MOTHER OF WHORES AND OF THE ABOMINATIONS OF THE EARTH."

Satan's Gang

Since satan does not honor God's Order his seed does not grow up through the orderly family pattern seen in the development of God's family. His 'family' is more of a gang than a family. Rather than love for Father God and respect for God's authority and His ways, independence and self-interest are the prime motivations. "What's in it for me?" is the slogan for satan's administration. That is why the main feature of world history under satan's rule is war—fueled by the struggle for power, material wealth and sensory gratification. Satan's seed are cut from the same cloth as their father. The ultimate goal is the consolidation of power—to control everything. The constant struggle and wrangling within satan's camp suits him just fine. It gives him the hook that he needs to control the greedy and power-hungry. He sought to ensnare even the Son of God with this hook, but he found no independent ambition there to hook into: "The devil took him to a very high mountain and showed him all the kingdoms of the world and their splendor. "All this I will give you," he said, "if you will bow down and worship me." Y'shua said to him, "Away from me, satan! For it is written: 'Worship YHWH your God, and serve him only.'" (Matthew 4:8-10)

Two Trees Planted At The Founding Of The World

The two families are like two trees planted in the earth at the founding of the world. This figure is found throughout the Scriptures, whether olive trees, figs or vines. The two trees are characterized by the two trees that God had put in the Garden. One tree, faithful Israel and her Seed, is nourished by and exhibits the Life of God. This is difficult, since all Adam's children—all mankind—have his life, anti-life, in them. This has caused some mutated and unwanted growth on God's tree. However, Father God has carefully pruned and cultivated His tree, and even injected it with His own Divine Life, that it might produce an abundant harvest of glory to Him.

The other tree, satan's world system, grows on the sap of selfish anti-life independence from God. It is a wild tree producing worthless fruit. And no wonder, for it exhibits the character of the life of its father! If it were not for God graciously grafting some of the branches from the wild tree onto His own tree it would serve little if any purpose at all. It's only other use is the usefulness of a bad example. For when the fruit of each becomes ripe and the day of harvest arrives the horrible fruit of satan's tree will only make the excellent fruit of God's tree stand out all the more for its glory. When that day comes even the usefulness of a bad example will pass and that awful tree will finally be put to the fire. Hallelujah!

The Fruit Will Tell The Story!

Is Father God's way right? Is it really love? Is submission to His authority, according to His order, right? Or is independence from God the way to go? Every intelligent creature in the universe must decide where he or she stands on these questions. Even those who are not consciously aware of the questions decide by their actions. Father YHWH shows the universe definitely which way is right by dealing with the rebellion through the principle of life and growth. A tree must produce fruit according to the life that is in it—"according to their kinds" as God had declared from the beginning. The fruit of the two trees would decide the issue forever, according to the principle clearly stated by the Son: "Every good tree bears good fruit, but a bad tree bears bad fruit. A good tree cannot bear bad fruit, and a bad tree cannot bear good fruit. Every tree that does not bear good fruit is cut down and thrown into the fire. Thus, by their fruit you will recognize them." (Matthew 7:17-20)

Oh, the depth of God's wisdom and knowledge! Even while Father God was passing judgment on the rebels—a judgment that brought a curse upon the earth and frustration and futility into the created world—He did so holding out hope of eventual victory over satan and all his works!

The Eternal Sovereign - An Estranged But Loving Father

Having considered God's judgment on the serpent let us now turn our attention back toward the man and women. Though God was choosing to allow satan's rule He was not abdicating His own. He had created the earth and it is His. His Sovereignty now and forever will be over all. God, though true to Himself in judging Adam and Eve, continued to act as a loving, if estranged, heavenly Father. Instead of leaving them exposed in their shame He clothed them in animal hides. In this He showed them that something would have to die for their shame to be covered. God thus pointed forward to the need for sacrifice. "... And YHWH God made coats of skin for the man and his wife and clothed them." (Genesis 3:20-21)

No Fellowship? ... Then No Life!

Independence from God and fellowship with God are antithetical. There is only One God. Man could not be a God to himself and at the same time live in fellowship with God. That would essentially elevate sinful man to the same level as God. This is simply not consistent with God's Order or God's nature as Father. Man had broken fellowship with God and was, therefore, no longer allowed to receive a daily supply of eternal life from the Tree of Life.

"And YHWH God said, Behold! The man has become as one of Us, to know good and evil. And now, lest he put forth his hand and also take from the Tree of Life, and eat, and live forever. And YHWH God sent him out of the Garden of Eden to till the ground out of which he was taken. And He drove the man out. And He caused to dwell the cherubs at the east of the Garden of Eden, and the flaming sword whirling around to guard the way of the Tree of Life." (Genesis 3:22-24)

Cast Out Of Paradise

God enforced his Word. He cast our first human parents out of the paradise to make their way in a hostile world. Then they would become painfully aware of the riches they had lost. They would want to go back. Their offspring would want to go back. They would lust after the Tree of Life—Not to be in fellowship with God—but to live in selfish independence from God and His order forever. For nearly two thousand years the Garden of Eden remained in place as a testimony of the Creator's love and man's glorious beginnings. All Adam's offspring could do was look at it longingly from the outside. God had placed powerful Cherubim with a whirling, flaming sword guarding the entrance to the Garden. No one would have eternal life apart from God's way! God's Order must be adhered to for God's life to flow. And so it is that a world divorced from Father God and God's Order came into being.

Answers For The Mystery Of The Shackle Dream

This brings us back to our launching point: the shackle dream. That shackle dream showed satan's seed, fallen mankind, slithering on their bellies in the dust of the earth. Now we know why. They are exhibiting the life of their serpentine father. They are shackled to a matrix that keeps them under his control - as slaves. Now we know how the crisscross matrix of the anti-life world system began to grow up to eventually cover the globe. We know how the master deceiver came to be the overlord of it all. And we know what the alternative is: Father God's Life and His Order flowing through the Son into God's family. Now we have the fundamentals. Let us move on to consider more carefully the development of the two alternatives. More importantly, let us move toward discovering the relevance of all this to us—the sons of God.

8

CREATION IN CRISIS

How cleverly the Enemy has discounted the truth of God's Word regarding the creation of man and the fall from human perfection in fellowship with Father God! Today few people believe these things ever really happened. Instead, the 'in thing' to believe is that by some unexplained accident of nature—perhaps a bolt of lightning striking a microscopic gob of pond scum—the upward evolution of mankind was begun. Never mind that this never happens in real life today. Never mind that this has not been and cannot be duplicated by scientific experimentation. It is, nonetheless, the accepted 'scientific' explanation of how life began. The alternative is to acknowledge accountability to the Creator. That, of course, is out of the question!

The Degeneration Of Man

The sad truth is that man is not evolving into something higher and better as the evolutionists and newagers would have us believe. In fact, the very opposite is true: Mankind is degenerating. With every passing generation we degrade farther from man's perfect beginnings. We delude ourselves when we believe that our technological advances are evidence that we are evolving into a "higher life form." These technological advances are merely the result of the applied accumulated knowledge of mankind. In other words, at this late date in human history we have all the research of earlier generations to benefit from. Each passing generation adds to that overall fund of knowledge—increasing our technological capabilities. While our knowledge of the natural world and ability to apply that knowledge has thus been increasing our basic humanity has not.

We have arrived at the point when we are technologically capable of doing things that we are not morally capable of controlling. Modern weaponry, including atomic, chemical and biological weapons, are a good example. We can kill and have killed countless more people more accurately and with greater ease than any of our 'barbaric' ancestors could have ever dreamed. This is higher evolution? And what of modern TV, video and audio capabilities? What about computers? All of these things are modern miracles with tremendous potential for good. However, I ask you, are these technologies used more to uplift the spirit and educate the mind—or to flood the senses with images of violence, lust and greed? If we were evolving upward our morality would be keeping pace with our technology. These few examples demonstrate that is not happening.

One shudders to think about what man might yet do through the manipulation of genetics—tampering with the very building blocks of biological life! The mastery of modern technology by degenerate mankind can only result in disaster for our planet and ourselves because degenerate mankind does not have the morality and wisdom to control such power.

Biological Superiority Of Early Man

The point we are beginning to stray from here is the absurdity of the claim that man is evolving upward. People of the first age of mankind lived to be hundreds of years old—some as old as 900+ years! This is no fairy tale. Those people were much closer to the human perfection of Eden than we are. Therefore their bodies simply lasted much longer than ours do. In fact, according to Dr. Jacob D. Liedmann, a neurosurgeon, the human body is capable of living about a thousand years if certain glands that once functioned continued to function today. According to neurosurgeon Liedmann, the pineal gland, located below the corpus callosum, has never functioned in modern man. It is believed to relate to the renewal of cell structure. Dr. Liedmann states; "Even though it doesn't appear to have any function today, its removal or the severing of connective tissue will result in death." The thymus is also believed to be the remains of a gland that once functioned with longevity benefits but now does not. Other glands that should continue to function with longevity benefits cease functioning early in life—with premature aging as the result. Liedmann states; "The key to life-spans like those mentioned in the Bible is within these glands." This is evidence within our own bodies that early man, while not yet having accumulated the scientific knowledge that we have today, was, nonetheless, biologically superior to us.[1]

Early Man Knew About Creation

Early human society knew where they had come from. The Garden of Eden remained in place for all to see—from the outside looking in. The Cherubim stood at the entrance to Eden with a supernatural flaming sword guarding the way to the Tree of Life. This silent testimony to Man's beginnings in Eden continued through the centuries until finally washed away in the Great Flood. Adam lived

930 years as a living testimony to that world of the Creator's reality. That generation knew the whole sad story of how perfection had been lost to them. This is born out through archaeological finds of artifacts of early civilization. For example, The Temptation Seal portrays a couple sitting beside a fruit-bearing tree with an upright serpent standing beside the woman, in a position as if whispering to her. She is depicted as reaching toward the fruit. The Adam and Eve Seal, dug up in 1932 from strata at Tepe Gawra near Nineveh, is also very telling. This ancient stone has an engraving of a dejected and fleeing naked man and woman followed by a serpent. It is a powerful illustration of the expulsion of our first parents from The Garden. Obviously, that expulsion had a major place in the consciousness of early human society.[2]

Genesis Is Recorded History!

The very construction of the book of Genesis reveals it to be real history. The first part of the book is the Creation Hymn. It was either given directly to Adam from God or was composed by Adam from what God had told him. This is not unlikely, since Adam was a ready poet and was in daily fellowship with God in Eden. This song was then passed down through the generations, much as we still sing the ancient ballads and hymns of our more recent ancestors. That Adam lived almost 1,000 years helped to insure that the original composition was accurately established and transmitted in the chosen family line. (Genesis 1:1-2:3)

The rest of the book of Genesis is actually a compilation of ten different genealogical documents recording family history and events relevant to family history. Each is called "The Generations of _____" These documents often contain some overlap of information, which is why Genesis, if read as a single book, sometimes appears to repeat itself. The documents include "The Generations of ... Adam ... Noah ... Sons of Noah, etc." The documents appear in chronological order, making up an unbroken history from the creation of man to the settlement of God's chosen family line in Egypt. It should be obvious to any student of these documents that they were highly treasured and therefore carefully and accurately preserved in the family line.[3]

Creation History Accurately Transmitted

The exceedingly long life span of early man aided accurate transmission of the Genesis documents. From the creation of Adam to Abraham, father of the Hebrew race, there are 20 generations. However, that 2,251 years is spanned by the lives of only three men: Adam, Methuselah and Shem. Adam lived over 200 years beyond the birth of Methuselah who was the eighth generation. Methuselah lived 98 years beyond the birth of Shem, the eleventh generation. Shem, born of pre-flood longevity, lived 600 years. That includes 150 years beyond the birth of Abram, the twentieth generation! That means Abram had access to eye witness confirmation of events going back before the Great Flood from Shem, a family forefather who had lived then and whose then living great-grandfather had himself lived since the time of Adam! Surely, this short chain of overlapping witnesses guaranteed the accurate transmission of the sacred family history. It's preservation as part of the Sacred Scriptures, carefully guarded through the centuries as a sacred trust from God by Father Abraham's faithful family line, insures it's accurate transmission even to the end of the age. Praise God for His precious Word of Truth!

A Written Record Of The First Man And His Family!

The first of the 'Generations' documents, following the Creation Hymn, is "The Generations of the Heavens and the Earth." We will call it GB2 for Genesis Book #2, the Creation Hymn being assigned the place of GB1. GB2 briefly comments on creation before Man, but the substance is on events from the creation of Man through to God's selection of Seth's line as the vessel of His choosing. The document also contains the contrasting history of the family of Cain. GB2 was probably originally written by Adam or largely dictated by Adam to Seth, who is the subject of the climax of the book. (Genesis 2:4-4:26)

Only Adam lived through the time span of the entire book. The brief history of the family of Cain stops with the eighth generation - the latest point in GB2. This is within Adam's lifetime, which continued to the ninth generation in the line of Seth. Further, (though written in the third person writing style) GB2 reads like a book written by a family head about the history of his family, especially when the original Hebrew is examined. The book is the known truth observed by Adam and received from God in the Garden, related from Adam's viewpoint. Ponder this: This is the historical account of Man #1 by Man #1! What do evolutionists have that can compete with that!

Having, then, this ancient historical document to draw from, and knowing that we are of the chosen family for whom this treasure has been preserved, let us confidently draw from its riches. Perhaps in doing so we too will be enlightened and empowered to take our place in God's plan as those before us have, to the praise of His Glory. With that end in mind let us resume our consideration of the great cosmic struggle that ensued after Man was expelled from paradise.

Who Was The Promised Seed?

In the preceding chapters we have been following the account of GB2 in its narration of the rebellion in Eden. We have seen that God's judgment of the rebels did not include their immediate destruction. Though we now have insight on the reason God did not destroy the rebels we must remember that they had no such insight. How shocked the Enemy must have been when he was allowed to roam free to be about his loathsome business! How shocked all heaven must have been! Satan would not waste time savoring his good fortune and his apparent success at founding an empire. He had work to do. Besides the expansion of his realm, his main goal would have to be the elimination of the promised Seed. If he could find a way to blot out that Seed his victory would be assured!

Of course, then the Enemy didn't know who the Seed of the Woman would be, or even who the Woman was, for that matter. God simply didn't say. GB2 implies that the rebels may have believed that Eve was the woman and Abel was the seed. At least this seems to be what Eve believed, when at the birth of Seth, she said: "God has appointed to me another seed in place of Abel, because Cain killed him." (Genesis 4:25b JPG)

Eve—and satan—may have believed Adam's son, Abel, to be the Seed because he was the first righteous man of Adam's offspring. Out of a pure, worshipful heart Abel sought fellowship with God through a sacrifice of the best of his flock. When his jealous brother, Cain, was not regarded with the same favor by God as was Abel, Cain murdered him—and this despite God's warning for Cain to get his spirit under control. This first murder set the pattern for the sea of righteous blood that would yet be shed upon the earth by the wicked.

We can read between the lines here and see that satan was working in Cain to destroy Abel, whom satan viewed as possibly being the Seed that would destroy him. All the better that he could eliminate Abel before he had any children to perpetuate a righteous family line! As Y'shua later said of satan; "He was a murderer from the beginning." Righteous Abel was not the promised Seed. He was, however, the first of a faithful remnant of humanity that would yet stretch through all the ages - set apart for Father God. The Lord had regard for Abel. (Genesis 4:1-4, John 8:44)

Satan's Seed Develops

As for Cain, God did not kill him. Further, God marked him that no one else would kill him either. Anyone who would kill him would be avenged sevenfold, God said. Cain's punishment was that the ground would be cursed toward him. Since he was a farmer this put an end to his livelihood. He became a fugitive in the land of Nod, which literally means 'wandering'. He likely took one of his sisters as a wife and she bore him a son, whom he named Enoch. Eventually Cain built the first city of human record and named it 'Enoch' after his son. How like satan that Cain sought to build an empire, establishing a dynasty in his son! It appears that in Cain satan had found a seed of his own through whom he could advance his own agenda of unseen control in the realm of men.

It was not long before there were more than enough people to populate that first city - then the world. The first of Adam's offspring were constrained to take wives from among their sisters. The first couple had a large family of both boys and girls from which the human race could multiply. The long life span of that day also impacted the numeric growth of the population astronomically. Imagine a childbearing lifespan of hundreds of years! Soon hundreds, then thousands, then millions, peopled the earth—more than enough to fill that first city and many more thereafter. (Genesis 5:4)

How Satan Perverted God's Order Of Authority

That first city must have had great influence in the lives of early civilization. It represents satan's first attempt at mass rule of mankind and offers a glimpse into his strategy of domination. God's plan had been for man to "multiply and fill the earth"—not gather in cities. City life fosters dictatorial and bureaucratic rule, abuse of God's creation, immorality and violence. A city is the opposite of the home God gave man in the Garden. Cities have great appeal to the anti-life nature. You might say, they are satan's candy store for the lower nature. The growth of wickedness in the earth must have been greatly hastened by the early establishment of city life through Cain. This was fundamental to satan's plan.

Remember, God had never given a hierarchical authority structure to man. God established patriarchal headship order among Mankind, which is family authority directly under God. Descending levels of authority characterized angelic life - not human life. As we shall see, it is very possible, in fact, likely, that materialized fallen angels were the ones to introduce the Godless system of hierarchical authority into the realm of men. The establishment of the first city represents satan's plan to pervert God's Order by patterning human society after that of the angels—but without God. Instead of God, satan would be the unseen top authority at the invisible level of the authority pyramid. In time there would be many such pyramids.[4]

Satan's Network Of Slavery Is Born!

Men were seduced into leaving the wide-open spaces in which they were free men to subject themselves to the government of the city. So doing, they were giving their own God-given authority over to the city government. In this way the legitimate self and family rule that God gave to men as their birthright became consolidated power in the hands of secular rulers—which they could use to oppress, coerce and to enrich themselves. Is this authority from God? Sadly, yes, even though it is a perversion of God's Order—because it originates in the authority He first gave to Man at Creation.

Why, though, did early men give up their God-given freedom to subject themselves to city rule? They were tempted by satan's candy store. Later generations, of course, knew nothing else. In this way the perversion became the norm. This perversion of God's Order puts satan in a position where he can use human government and culture to exercise great control over practically every aspect of human life. It is diabolical and dehumanizing in the extreme.

This ties in directly with the shackle dream. With the ungodly culture and human government of the first city satan began his construction of the crisscross network by means of which he could shackle men's minds. His goal has always been that none should be free to obey God. He will not rest till all are shackled to his instrument of oppression and control.

More About Cain's Family Line

Just a few more words about Cain's family line. Cain's descendant of the seventh generation, Lamech, claimed to have killed a man in self-defense. This seems to indicate the escalation of violence on the earth by that day. Lamech is often said to have originated polygamy since this is the first mention of it in Scripture. However, the text does not support that assumption. Matter-of-factly GB2 states that "Lamech took two wives" - not that he was the first to do so. It goes on to speak of his sons, whom it calls, respectively, the "father of" those who play musical instruments, work metal and herd cattle. It would have been consistent for the verse to say that Lamech was the "father of" those taking multiple wives, if that had been the case. Actually, the casual way in which the text deals with Lamech's two wives seems to indicate that was not uncommon then, as also throughout Genesis. (Genesis 4:19-24, 25:6, 28:9, 30:26, 32:22, 36:2)

A Righteous Planting In The Earth For God's Name

The story of Cain and his family line well illustrates the hatred of the Serpent's seed for God's Order and God's righteous chosen line. However, GB2 does not leave us believing that God's plan of Genesis 3:15 was defeated with the death of righteous Abel and the spread of wickedness in the earth. Rather, the book ends with the righteous planting of Seth's line taking root in the earth.

We are told that God gave Seth in place of righteous Abel. The stage for the closing verse is set with the perpetuation of Seth's line through the birth of his son, Enosh. With Seth's line thus established GB2 climaxes with the words: "Then it was begun to call on the name of YHWH." (Genesis 4:25-26 JPG)

The point is that through Seth a righteous family line had been established in the earth "to call on the name of YHWH." Father God had set apart a chosen family line for His Name, through which He would work His will in the earth—even eventually producing the promised Seed. HalleluYah!

"The Book of the Generations of Adam" gives the history of the family line through Seth, which line was set apart by God in GB2. In other words, this is a history of the chosen family line, from Adam to Noah and Noah's sons. GB3 begins with a brief narration of information already covered in GB2, including information about the creation of Adam and the birth of Seth. This information would have been largely unnecessary if GB3 had not originally been a separate book—clearly indicating that it had been. It is likely that this document was passed down through the generations with each generation adding the genealogical information about the immediately preceding generation. In this way an accurate chronology from the creation of man to the birth of Noah's sons was recorded and passed down. The last person mentioned is Noah, still alive at the age of five hundred years. That fact makes it likely that Noah was the final author of GB3. (Genesis 5:1-6:8, here following as GB3)

God's Order After The Fall

Both GB2 and GB3, are decidedly patriarchal throughout. We have already seen God's patriarchal order before the fall. As a result of the fall from perfection life was hard and marriage diminished in quality from the original design. Sin had raised a barrier between men and their Head. This caused the headship of men over women to be degenerate, as was also the submission of wives to their husbands. Nevertheless, Patriarchal Order remained as a reflection of God's original plan in Eden. This is evidenced by the fact that the recorded genealogies of Adam's sons, Cain and Seth, are unmistakably patriarchal in nature, listing only fathers and sons in the lists of 'begats' This patriarchal orientation continues throughout all the books of Genesis. (Genesis 4:16-5:2).

Enoch - First To Walk With God

The 'begats' go to the seventh generation before anyone in the family line progressed from 'calling on the name of YHWH' to actually 'walking with God.' Enoch was the seventh generation starting with Adam, through Adam's son, Seth. Due to the great lifespan of those days both Adam and Seth were still alive in Enoch's day. Enoch "walked with God." To "walk with God" implies intimate fellowship with God and submission to God throughout the daily affairs of Enoch's life. God was the real Head of Enoch. This is the primary requirement of fundamental Headship Order.

Enoch's walk with God brought him into conflict with the society of his age. It seems that the people of that world had come to see God as too kind or too slow to bring punishment for evil. After all, God had not destroyed the rebels in the Garden. He did not destroy Cain for the murder of Abel. He apparently was doing nothing about the wickedness of Cain's city or other cities founded later. This attitude—mistaking the patience of God for weakness toward evil—tempted both men and angels to moral license. If God would not execute judgment against wickedness then one could do whatever one pleased without fear of real punishment. How this affected angels we shall see later. Its effect upon men was to draw out their hearts, for when there is no fear of punishment what a man is at heart cannot be hidden. Those with loyal hearts remain loyal. Those with hidden wickedness in their hearts give vent to evil. With the exception of the loyal Enoch and his family, it was an evil age. (See 2 Peter 3:1-10)

God raised up Enoch as a prophet against the majority. He may have been named the same as Enoch, the city of Cain, because his prophetic message was meant to be directed toward that center of evil. In any event, scornful humans needed to know that they were wrong—God would judge wickedness. The warning from God would kindly allow any who so desired to repent in God's fear and be saved from that evil generation: "Enoch, the seventh from Adam, prophesied about these men: "See, YHWH is coming with thousands upon thousands of his holy ones to judge everyone, and to convict all the ungodly of all the ungodly acts they have done in the ungodly way, and of all the harsh words ungodly sinners have spoken against him."" (Jude 14,15 NIV)

As far as we know, none other than family took Enoch's message seriously. Enoch was a misfit—a righteous man in an unrighteous age. He stood alone in the world—but not alone—he walked with God. The conflict between his righteous soul and the evil that was running rampant was so great that he could not bear it. At the abnormally early age of 365 years God kindly took him home without seeing death to spare his righteous soul the torment of enduring that licentious society. (Genesis 5:18-24, Hebrews 11:5, Jude 14,15)

Enoch - Patriarch Of God's One Family In All The Earth!

Enoch was a faithful Patriarchal head of the chosen line. No doubt, this was evidenced in Enoch's loving headship of his family. I say this because Enoch would have had access to the family history and understood God's Patriarchal Order. As we have noted, the family genealogy (GB3), recording as it does the family line through the fathers and sons and recording God's dealings with those men, is a patriarchal document written from a patriarchal point of view. Therefore, Enoch, included in that patriarchal document, was himself a patriarch. As a man who walked with God Enoch was equipped to be an outstanding family head. For one can only practice Godly headship after one has first learned Godly submission - and submission is what "walking with God" is all about.

Enoch's outstanding headship is revealed by its good fruit. Methuselah, Enoch's son, was granted the longest life of human record - 969 years. No doubt this blessing fell upon Methuselah because of YHWH's regard for the faithfulness of his father. Methuselah's son, Enoch's grandson, Lamech, was a prophet of God like his grandfather, Enoch. His life overlapped with that of Enoch by over 100 years. Lamech passed on the family birthright to his son, whom he named Noah (meaning rest or consolation). When naming his son, Lamech prophesied that the curse of the ground would be lifted through him. This later proved to be true, as we shall see. (Genesis 5:28-31, 8:21)

In Enoch the tender shoot of God's righteous planting in the earth had been strengthened to a formerly unprecedented perfection of faith - even in the face of a darkening cloud of wickedness. Enoch's line would prove to be at once God's only vehicle for preserving His own Cause and the race of man on the earth. This is the wonder of our Father. Not that He asks us to trust Him—for He is ever trustworthy—but that He puts full and absolute trust in His own! He had narrowed down the whole race of man to one family line that He had set apart for Himself. Finally, after seven generations, He had totally captured one man's heart. Oh, the wonder of it! Could that same depth of commitment be passed on to Enoch's descendants? That would prove to be a vital question, since God's Eternal Purpose and the very survival of the human creation would stand or fall on the strength of the integrity of one man in that chosen family line.

Fallen Angel's Pervert God's Order To Advance Satan's Plan

By the time of Enoch's prophetic message nearly a millennium had passed without any apparent action on God's part against wayward mankind or against satan. Although Genesis does not speak directly of satan, later Scripture would lead us to believe that satan had long since taken his campaign of rebellion into heaven itself. No doubt it was suggested by satan to the angels of God that God's 'bark was worse than His bite'—that God could be disobeyed without real punishment. Then, such a claim seemed to be true. Further, we can be sure that satan's siren song of independence from God first sung in the Garden was endlessly repeated in the realm of heaven. This message was given added force by the fact that satan's plan of domination in the earth seemed to be succeeding beyond his wildest dreams. With the exception of one no-account family the whole earth was following after him! This must have been very impressive to many of the angels. Later Scripture indicates that a large fraction of the heavenly host chose to throw their lot in with the silver-tongued Deceiver. These fallen angels are later referred to as 'demons' in the Scriptures. (2 Peter 3, Revelation 12: 3-4)

Some of those angels actually forsook their proper place in God's Order to cohabit with women. The first recorded adultery—and that of a grossly perverse sort—is here: "The sons of God (angels) saw that the daughters of men were beautiful; and they took women for themselves, whomever they chose." (Genesis 6:2 'Sons of God' Job 1:6, 2:1 etc.)

God had given the angels the ability to assume human-like material bodies so that they would be able to interact in the physical world as His messengers to men. However, their proper dwelling place is in heaven as spirits. Further, angels were never intended to marry and reproduce. However, some rebel angels forsook their proper place and abused their ability to take on material form to cohabit with women. Angels are much more powerful than humans. In taking 'whomever they chose' they apparently did so without regard to human will. If they wanted a man's wife they had superior strength to take her, whether she or her husband objected or not, thus committing adultery against the human husband (and possibly violence against both). Of course, they also took single women and girls for whom they had equal disregard.

That fallen angels (demons) are here demonstrated in Scripture to have a debased sexual lust is a frightening thought. It is, however, a Biblical fact and accounts for the perverse sexual rites that inevitably accompany every spiritistic pagan religion down through history. Pagan religions often report sexual relations between women and 'gods'. There is more to this than mere myth.

It is not just the sex that is the object of the demons. "They took women for themselves" - i.e., through sexual relations they gained headship authority over women. It is this authority, exercised apart from the loving headship God intended, that they delight in. Headship authority is a real spiritual force imbued with the power inherent in God's Order. Through perversion of God's natural order fallen angels took control over the human will of women. The bonus for them in this is, as with Eve, through control of women wicked spirits can control men.

Wicked Demon Seed Perverts God's Order

These unions between angels and women were a terrible perversion of God's natural order, producing hybrid mutant offspring that were far mightier than ordinary men. These unnatural super-human giants were called 'Nephilim'—the 'mighty men...of renown.' One of these giants was reported to be over nine feet tall! The name Nephilim comes from a root meaning to 'cause to fall,' to 'cast down.' Certainly this name suggests violence. Beyond brute violence, though, it suggests dominance by force. Renown (literally meaning "name") suggests position and authority—authority from their angelic fathers. In other words, it was through angels establishing their Nephilim sons in authority in the cities that the angelic hierarchical government first made its way from heaven into the earth. The Nephilim established and enforced their authority over men through oppression and violence. Thus, they became "the mighty men of renown"—the ruling class on earth. Given the dominant nature of the Nephilim, and given enough unrestrained time, they would certainly have supplanted men altogether. The influence of the Nephilim plunged the entire world into grievous wickedness and violence to the extent that virtually the whole human race was utterly ruined beyond the point of repair. (Genesis 6:4)

In this evil strategy satan was again using women to pervert God's natural order. Sex with fallen angels rather than men would eventually totally corrupt the human blood line that was to lead to the promised Seed—the man who would crush satan's head. This brilliantly wicked scheme was really a preemptive attack to prevent the dreaded 'Seed of the woman' from ever being born! (2 Peter 2:4-5, Jude 6)

It All Comes Down To One Man

The situation was dire. God's natural order had literally been turned upside down so that God's work in the earth was utterly ruined. Faced with the corruption of the human race, which had been greatly hastened by the fallen angels and their Nephilim offspring, God was left with no alternative but to wipe the earth clean. Nothing short of that would be sufficient to the situation. God's heart was grieved as He set a limit of 120 more years before He would have to destroy it all.

Surely, I must be exaggerating. Man could not have become totally evil in less than only two millennia, could he? Read it for yourself: "YHWH saw that the evil of man was great on the earth, and every imagination of the thoughts of his heart was only evil all the day long. And YHWH repented that He had made man on the earth, and He was grieved to His heart. And YHWH said, "I will wipe off man whom I have created from the face of the earth, from man to beast, to creeping thing and to the bird of the heavens; for I repent that I made them.""" (Genesis 6:5-7)

Dear brother, do you feel God's pain of heart, as I do, when you read that? Our Father is not speaking out of wrath, but out of acknowledgment of the sorry truth of the situation, when He determines that the earth must be wiped clean.

Does this mean YHWH was defeated? Never. He had kept one man for Himself. He had no back-up man. No plan 'B' man. It would be satan and his whole wicked world on one side and God and His man on the other.

Thus GB3 ends with the words: Noah found grace in the eyes of YHWH. Genesis 6:8

FOOTNOTES:

[1]. Statements made by Dr. Jacob D. Liedmann during a March 1976 interview and reported in *The Incredible Discovery Of Noah's Ark* by Sellier & Balsiger, (New York: Dell, 1995) pp 120-121. There is scientific evidence suggesting that the pre-flood world enjoyed a pressurized oxygen-rich atmosphere with nearly total protection from the harmful extraterrestrial radiation that we experience today, along with other beneficial atmospheric conditions. These factors likely played a role in the longevity of early man also. For more information see Frederick A. Filby, *The Flood Reconsidered* (Grand Rapids: Zondervan Corp., 1971), Henry M. Morris, *Scientific Creationism* (San Diego: Creation-Life Publishers, 1974)

[2]. Henry H. Halley. *Halley's Bible Handbook*, (Grand Rapids: Zondervan Corp., 1965) pp 68.

[3]. Henry H. Halley. *Halley's Bible Handbook*, (Grand Rapids: Zondervan Corp., 1965) pp 58-59.

[4]. There is much to suggest that the fallen angels had a great deal to do with the social structure and scientific advances of pre-flood civilization. Ancient writers, based on what they accepted as earlier pre-flood writings, attribute much associated with early city life to fallen angels. For Example, Tertullian, an early Christian writer [140-230 A.D.], states: "...For when these fallen angels had revealed certain well-hidden material substances, and numerous other arts that were only faintly revealed, to an age much more ignorant than ours--for surely they are the ones who disclosed the secrets of metallurgy, discovered the natural properties of herbs, made known the power of charms, and aroused the desire to pry into everything, including the interpretation of the stars...etc" (Book 1, Chapter 2, Section 1). Modern man is faced with some amazing puzzles from the pre-flood era. For example, how could those ancient people cut and move 200 ton stones to form ancient structures? Yet we know they did because some of those structures still exist. How could they produce metal alloys that even modern science cannot reproduce? - For example, the bell found encased in coal from deep beneath the earth by a chemist named Newton Anderson, who describes it thus; "The bell has an unusual pagan god on top of the stem with both arms and wings raised upward." Anderson had an electron elemental analysis test done to determine the elemental composition of the bell. It was found to be of a metallurgical composition so unusual that it could not be reproduced by today's technology! Similar results have been obtained in testing other very ancient metal objects. These puzzles are solved if we accept the ancient wisdom regarding the influence of fallen angels in the pre-flood world. See *The Incredible Discovery Of Noah's Ark* by Sellier & Balsiger, (New York: Dell, 1995) pp 95-98.

9

GOD'S ORDER TRIUMPHS!

Satan's conceit likely deluded him into believing he had defeated God. His scheme was working perfectly. Many angels had defected over to his side. Angels taking women were defiling the very seed of man. The earth's entire population, excepting one oddball family, had entirely turned away from YHWH. It would just be a matter of time before any possibility of the promised 'Seed' emerging would be totally eliminated. Satan's perversion of God's Order as the weapon of God's defeat was wickedly brilliant. Through all of this YHWH seemed to be doing nothing—as if His creation had moved beyond His Sovereign control. Seeing this, more angels kept defecting to satan's side—perhaps up to a third of the heavenly host in all! How could the Almighty let this happen? Had He really been caught unawares?

Not a chance! Father YHWH had foreseen it all. He only wants willing servants. It was in His interest that those angels who didn't value their service to Him as their highest treasure—It was in His interest and ours that those ingrates should show themselves up for what they really were! God's patience served the purpose of allowing all the heavenly host who would desert to do so. Meanwhile, those that remained had been given the opportunity to prove themselves faithful—worthy of their high privilege of serving Him.

God's Man Was The Key

As for the wickedness of man, God's heart was deeply grieved. However, there was a purpose served by that too. That wicked world was like a fire in God's hand that forged the heart of His servant Noah into hardened steel for YHWH! In the man, Noah, YHWH had turned the whole tragic situation into a backdrop against which His glory revealed in Noah and Noah's family shone forth like the sun against the black of space. Satan's weapon, namely the perversion of God's Order, surely had overwhelmed the earth. There could be no doubt of that. But it had not overwhelmed God. For YHWH had a perfect plan to put the world back on track. Noah was the key to God's plan in that day—God's man—a prepared vessel for a very special purpose. The great cosmic struggle between satan's strategy of God's Order Perverted versus God's Order Obeyed thus narrowed down to the life of that one man, Noah. The name, Noah, means "peace" because in him the mounting tension between the two great forces would find its inevitable release—bringing the calm of a new day wherein the truth had been proved out. Let us now examine the life and times, "The generations of Noah [GB4]."

God's Vessel Prepared Through His Order

"These are the generations of Noah. Noah, a righteous man, had been perfected among his family [line]—Noah walked with God." (Genesis 6:9 JPG [brackets mine])

As this verse reminds us, God was not desperately searching around for a man that He could use in that hour. According to His way of working through life and growth He had been perfecting a family line that belonged to Him. Noah's great-grandfather, Enoch, was the first of that line to have moved past merely calling on the name of YHWH to actually walking with God. As a pioneer Enoch had made the way and walked alone. That courageous lone-prophet walked with YHWH right out of this world into the next. In his day it must have appeared that he had actually accomplished nothing - having no repentant converts to show for his ministry. Yet, his faithfulness was not lost on his family. The Life of God that had been produced in Enoch grew up ever stronger in his family line leading to Noah. Enoch's son, Methuselah, and Methuselah's son Lamech (who was Noah's father), carried the faith of Enoch forward to Noah. Lamech was alive to teach, guide and support his son, Noah, up to the 595th year of Noah's life, dying of old age only five years before the Great Flood. Methuselah, Noah's grandfather, died of extreme old age (969 years) as the oldest man who ever lived in the very year of the Great Flood. Thus, Noah had the benefit of Godly support and the counsel of righteous fathers throughout his pre-flood ministry.

That Noah was righteous, then, was no accident. It's how he was raised. YHWH had created a family environment with a proud family history of faith that was the trunk producing the fruit of Noah's growth in God. Not only that, but Noah was made to be the repository of that family history stretching back to the creation of the world. Noah knew God's ways and conformed his life to God's Order. The faithful men of YHWH in his family line set the Godly example and, no doubt, offered needed correction, especially during his formative years. God's patriarchal order, then, is seen to have been God's primary weapon against satan's evil scheme. Through God's patriarchal order "Noah was perfected in his family line."

Noah - Righteous In His Time

To live God's way in that generation must have been considered not only crazy—but also dangerous. How is it that Noah could live in a way totally opposed to his time and not be killed or buckle under to societal pressure? It was not because he just 'didn't rock the boat'—didn't tell anyone the truth. On the contrary, Noah was a "preacher of righteousness" in his age. In effect, Noah dared to say; "I'm right and the world is wrong." Noah was right and the world was wrong! The only explanation for the fact that satan and the world were unable to eliminate Noah, (the only threat to them in the whole earth) was because God "preserved Noah, a preacher of righteousness." (Hebrews 11:7, 1 Peter 2:5)

Even with his uniquely solid family background the pressure to succumb to an ungodly life in that wicked world must have been monumental. So the question remains: How could Noah live in a way totally opposed to the ways of his time and not buckle under to the prodigious social pressure? It was only possible because "Noah walked with God." Consider what that means. Noah belonged to no church or denomination. Noah had no Bible or religious creed as such - although he did have the record of God's dealings with man recorded in his family line up until his time. What Noah had received as his great family legacy along with that record was a personal relationship with YHWH—fellowship with God. Noah knew his place in God's Order. He submitted his life unreservedly to the Lord's authority as his Head. He obeyed YHWH. Noah knew God...Talked with God...Heard God speak to him. Obeyed what he heard on a daily basis. Noah lived in intimate day-by-day fellowship and dependence on a personal living God—Noah walked with God. This is how Noah could be righteous in a decidedly unrighteous age. This is how Noah could be sure that he was right and the whole world was wrong—How he could be sure of God's mind expressed to him personally—Because he walked with God. Not because he was religious, but because he actually walked with God. Get it?!

It was because Noah actually walked with God that YHWH could say to Noah; "I have seen you righteous before Me in this generation [meaning: in Noah's time]." (Genesis 7:1 JPG)

Transcend Your Time!

When you think about it, walking with God as Noah did is the only way to be 'righteous in your time'. The natural way of things, otherwise, is that we are all a product of our time. We think and do very much what we are programmed to think and do by the influences of the generation we live in. Work, family life, moral standards—even religion and Biblical interpretation are seen through a lens of mental conditioning reflecting the beliefs and societal attitudes of our generation. Thus viewed, even what we are sure is 'right' cannot be trusted as what God sees as 'right' in a given situation. Only by walking with God—knowing Him, talking to Him, hearing Him and obeying Him—can we be sure that what we are doing or not doing is truly 'right' as far as God is concerned. There is a perfect consistency to God and God's Order that is eternal and therefore transcends the mindset of every age. If we walk with Him He can lift our thinking above the level of our time to conform our lives to the Eternal Order.

Here we should be reminded that there is a cost attached to such transcendence. If one would be righteous in his time he must be determined to care more for what YHWH thinks than for the opinions of those around him. Talking to and hearing God sounds crazy to a world estranged from its Creator. Living this way often creates suspicion and misunderstanding in the minds of those who do not know God—resulting in vilification and/or persecution of God's man. I know of what I speak. This writer was once ordered by a court of law to submit to a professional psychological evaluation because of hearing and obeying God. It was quite baffling for officials when that evaluation proved this writer mentally sound rather than crazy! Hearing God is not as crazy as the world thinks. If anyone is really serious about it all they need do is surrender their entire life to Him, becoming a fool to the world, as Noah did. Then God will talk to them. If you're not willing to do that then don't expect to be hearing from YHWH—because you are not acting in a manner worthy of His attention.

On Track With God

In that sense, Noah was worthy, so God spoke to him: " A n d God said to Noah, The end of all flesh has come before Me...Make an ark...I am bringing a flood of waters on the earth in order to destroy all flesh." (Genesis 6:13-21 JPG)

See here the alternative to the matrix system that holds the mass of humanity in blind servitude to the demands of human thought and culture—even as it did in Noah's day. While the whole world partied ignorantly on toward destruction Noah lived and moved in a higher place—in God. Thus Noah alone was in sync with the flow of God's created world and the events about to move from the unseen into the natural—having been brought into God's intimate counsel. Noah was on a different track than the rest of his generation. He was walking on God's track with God. Whatever might be ahead, Noah was on the right track to deal with it. Walking with God according to the pattern of His Eternal Order is the only way to transcend the brain chains of this world! Messiah reminds us of exactly this contrast between the world and Noah and says that the same pattern will be evident at His soon return. Let us be wise and learn from this: "For in the days before the flood, people were eating and drinking, marrying and giving in marriage, up to the day Noah entered the ark; and they knew nothing about what would happen until the flood came and took them all away. That is how it will be at the coming of the Son of Man." (Matthew 24:38-39 NIV)

While the world was selfishly oblivious to the impending doom, God told Noah exactly what was about to happen. There would be a worldwide flood that would destroy every creature on the surface of the earth. Noah was not left to figure out what to do about the impending catastrophe. God told Noah exactly what to do and how to do it. The project, outlined in detail by YHWH, was huge. Noah, with the help of his wife, his three sons, Shem, Ham and Japheth, and their wives, was to build a watertight wooden ark [meaning a simple box or chest, not the popular conception of a boat] three stories high and about 450 feet long with room enough for two of every kind of land animal on earth! There must have been a rather unusual discussion around the Noah family table the night Noah revealed this! When people today hear the Noah account they ask, how could all those animals fit in the ark? How could they all dwell together in peace? Where did the water come from? Where did it go? ...and blah, blah, blah...every question suggesting doubt that there ever was a Great Flood. There are satisfactory answers to every question. However, that is not the point of this book. The point here is this: Noah and his family entertained no such doubts. Their trust in God and His Word through Noah was complete. Their very lives—and ours—depended on it.[1]

Noah And His Family Blessed Through God's Order

Here again we see God working according to His patriarchal order. God spoke to the Family head, Noah - assuming Noah would have the total support of his wife and sons. Noah, in turn, passed on God's instructions to his family and directed the project to conform exactly to God's commands. Noah would be the one who would have to answer to God, so "Noah did everything just as God commanded him." Thus God's patriarchal order was God's channel of communication and direction to accomplish His perfect will in that day. That order produced a unity of purpose and effort within the family that would be sustained for the best part of one hundred years—until the gigantic project was completed exactly according to God's specifications.[2] (Genesis 6:22 NIV)

Four Keys To Success

Three keys to that success were faith, submission and obedience. Noah's faith in God's message and his submission and obedience to God were fundamental—then the submission and obedience of Noah's family to Noah's delegated authority as family head, which also implies faith in both God and Noah. There is no record of anyone in Noah's family questioning God's commands through Noah or refusing to cooperate in any aspect of the building project. Without such remarkable faith, submission and obedience, family discord surely would have been satan's means of thwarting God's plan. That indicates a fourth key—love. For without love oiling the rough spots during the grueling project family unity certainly would have broken down. God's men—are you and your family striving toward functioning like that? Remember, as the head of your family it all starts with you.

The Superiority Of God's Ways

Contrast what YHWH accomplished through His patriarchal order in Noah's family to what would have happened if 'modern' ideas of family structure had been followed. A 'modern' wife would have said; "if this message is really from God why didn't He tell me, too, since we're equal partners in this relationship? Who do you think you are to tell me I need to focus all my attention on helping you build a 450 foot box! Get real! I have a career to think about. I can't just drop all my aspirations as an individual to involve myself with your crazy building project"! Then the sons might have said something like; "We have our future to think about, Dad. And besides, our wives will never go for this. It will embarrass them too much with their family and friends. Good luck, though!" At about that point Noah, being God's man, would have said something like; "For your sake I hope you change your minds. Meanwhile, I had better get to work!" Providentially, Noah's family was not like that. They respected the lines of Godly blessing and authority that came to them through the family patriarch. That respect saved their lives. Let us learn from Messiah's warning and the example of Noah's family. Like Noah, we must pattern our lives and families according to God's Order to fit ourselves for usefulness in God's plan—for God's people are still the center of His purposes on this earth.

A Perverse World Washed Away

We need not elaborate greatly on the details of the flood story. You should read it for yourself. It reads very credibly like a captain's log of events. We know that the ark was built and stocked with food. We know that at the appointed time God brought two of every land animal and seven of every sacrificial animal into the ark. Seven days before God would bring the flood God commanded Noah and his family, a total of eight souls, to enter the ark. With no hesitation they left that world behind to move on with God. We can only imagine the sense of anticipation and exhilaration they must have felt at the beginning of that transition from one world to another. When all were aboard, "God shut the door." In all of this we are twice told that "Noah did according to all that YHWH had commanded him." (Genesis 6:22, 7:5 JPG)

For seven days Noah and his family waited inside the ark for the flood to begin. It was a good opportunity for Noah and his family to get acquainted with all the animals, with whom they enjoyed a supernatural peace. Outside the world was going on as it, seemingly, always had. It must have seemed like a very long week. We can imagine the scoffers making fun of Noah and the ark as the week was passing by. Their worldly mindset simply could not fathom the spectacle. After the seven appointed days they were scoffing no more, for God's time had expired on that wicked world![3] Satan's perverted world order, which had seemed so formidable and permanent, was wiped away by God as easily as a man washes a dirty dish: "In the six hundredth year of Noah's life, in the second month, in the seventeenth day of the month, in this day all the fountains of the great deep were risen, and the windows of the heavens were opened up...And the flood was on the earth forty days. And the waters increased on the earth. And the ark floated on the face of the waters. And the waters were strong, exceedingly violent on the earth, and all the high mountains were covered...And every living thing which was on the face of the earth was wiped away...And they were wiped off from the earth, and only Noah was left, and those who were with him in the ark." (Genesis 7:11-24 JPG)

The Triumph Of God's Way Over Wicked Spirits

Thus, God wiped the wickedness of man off the earth. At the same time he preserved pure the race of man from the corruption of the Nephilim, who were destroyed in the flood. Neither were the wicked angels that had corrupted the earth through abandoning their appointed places in heaven able to escape God's judgment. Although they were able to escape the flood by dematerializing into their spirit bodies they were not able to flee from the Creator, whose power and gaze pervades every corner of the universe. Even now these woeful spirits are enchained in a spiritual prison, awaiting the Day of Judgment, at which time they will receive the just punishment for their treasonous crimes against God and His Eternal Order. The Scriptures make this plain: "Those angels not having kept their first place, but having deserted their dwelling place [in heaven], He has kept in everlasting chains under darkness for the judgment of the great Day." (Jude 6 JPG, Peter 2:4-5, 1 Peter 3:19-20)

Wicked Spirits Still Roam - With Limits

While the spirits that have physically defiled women must endure the bonds of prison, the rest of the angels who defected to satan's side have been allowed to continue to roam freely. They are identified in Scripture as the devil's angels—as demons. As the heavenly part of satan's seed they are at enmity with God and God's Woman and are given freedom according to God's judgment in Eden to develop and promote satan's program of rebellion. This is in keeping with God's perfect decision to settle the Great Controversy through allowing both sides to grow to maturity, at which time the issue will be eternally settled. However, with the Flood and the imprisonment of the angels that sinned, Father God demonstrated that there are limits to what He will allow until then. He has not abdicated His Throne and He is free to judge wickedness where and when He determines that it is called for. As Sovereign, He simply will not allow the wholesale perversion and mutation of the seed of man by human cohabitation with materialized spirits. God's judgment at the Flood proves that Father God will act to protect the natural order from any permanent and fundamental damage.

It is certain that this point has not been lost on satan's demons. From the Flood forward they know that if they cross the line they risk immediate and certain imprisonment—the example of the punishment befalling the pre-flood sinning angels being the surety for that boundary. This seems to be the reason that the materialization of wicked spirits and human cohabitation with them has been a rare, though not a nonexistent, occurrence in the post Flood world. I say that because it appears that some fallen angels have risked the penalty at key points in satan's strategy. That fact will be illuminated as we progress to specific examples of which we speak. However, the wholesale materialization of demons throughout the earth that so accelerated the wickedness of man before the Flood would never be allowed to happen again. Thus, the progression of wickedness towards its fullness has not been so swift in the post Flood world.

Scoffers Deny God

It has now been thousands of years since the Great Flood. Although there is abundant proof that it occurred our 'scientific' generation would rather avoid the implications of such proof by denying the reality of the Flood. So when they find seashells on mountaintops it was not the Flood that deposited them there—it was the 'ice age.' Even the discovery of the ark itself is insufficient proof for the sophisticated scoffers. That's right, the discovery of the ark itself! It remains preserved in the glacier on the mountains of Ararat and has been seen by scores of people over the ages—many during the twentieth century. It has been measured, photographed and studied. Its location is well known to the world's superpowers, since they have satellite photos pinpointing and confirming its exact location! It was reportedly by using such government information that U. S. Astronaut Jim Erwin obtained an aerial photo of the ark that is still available for all to see![1]

Scoffers say that the Flood is just a myth. They don't want to believe that the Sovereign God will soon judge this wayward world as He once did by the Flood. But make no mistake, the prophecy of Enoch and all the faithful prophets that God's Son will come with His holy angels to judge this world will come true without fail. It must come true because God's Word cannot fail. The Flood stands as proof for all time that YHWH will judge wickedness, whether the scoffers believe it or not. It is ironic that their scoffing is the very proof of the nearness of that judgment, even as has been prophesied: "knowing this first, that in the last days mockers will come, walking after their own lusts, and saying, "Where is the promise of his coming? For, from the day that the fathers fell asleep, all things continue as they were from the beginning of the creation." For this they willfully forget, that there were heavens from of old, and an earth formed out of water and amid water, by the word of God; by which means the world that then was, being overflowed with water, perished. But the heavens that now are, and the earth, by the same word have been stored up for fire, being reserved against the day of judgment and destruction of ungodly men. But don't forget this one thing, beloved, that one day is with the Lord as a thousand years, and a thousand years as one day. The Lord is not slow concerning his promise, as some count slowness; but is patient with us, not wishing that any should perish, but that all should come to repentance." (2 Peter 3:3-9)

How kindhearted is our God! He is slow to bring judgment so that everyone who chooses to may come to repentance. What a mistake, to consider God's patience as meaning that judgment will never come! This is exactly the same foolish mistake that was made by that ancient pre-Flood world! What a sad lost opportunity!

God's Men - Hasten The Day!

Dear brother, do not miss the profundity of this truth. God's judgment is hastening forward. In fact, we His own are called upon to hasten it even as the faithfulness of Noah can be thought of as hastening the Flood. Listen: "By faith, Noah, being warned about things not yet seen, moved with godly fear, prepared an ark for the saving of his house, through which he condemned the world, and became heir of the righteousness which is according to faith." (Hebrews 11:7)

Even as Noah's holy and righteous faith cooperated with God's plan to hasten it—condemning the world and saving mankind—so now God is calling upon us to do the very same. Take this in: "Since everything will be destroyed in this way [by God's judgment fire], what kind of people ought you to be? You ought to live holy and godly lives as you look forward to the day of God and SPEED ITS COMING." (2 Peter 3:11, 12 NIV)

SPEED ITS COMING...SPEED ITS COMING...SPEED ITS COMING!...Brothers, we can speed the coming of that day! Too long have God's men seen themselves as mere spectators, waiting for God's predetermined day of salvation and judgment. That's the passive, unengaged, spiritually lazy and simply wrong mindset! We are not called to be spectators of God's plan - like Noah; we are called to be enablers of that plan! Get with the program. As God's man God is depending on you to do your part. Ask your Father to help you grow up into the true manhood required by God's Order and exemplified by Noah. Right now God's plan requires men like that.

A Supernatural Lesson

This message strikes an important cord for me, since the Lord Y'shua first impressed it on me in a supernatural way. Not long after He first called me to this ministry, back in 1981, he gave me a profound vision of His Coming. I remember the exact date because it was the same day as the assassination of Anwar Sadat of Egypt, October 6, 1981. I had just seen breaking news of that assassination on TV and was alone and wide-awake in a room of my home when the Lord impressed these moving images on my mind. It was as if I was looking through the black of space to see the King of Kings and His heavenly armies riding on white horses toward the earth. My perspective was from a distance where I could see the earth as a blue marble suspended in space. The Lord was riding in front with the heavenly host stretching out behind. They were descending in a great spiral toward the earth! Suddenly my perspective changed and

I saw and felt that I was mounted on a white horse, riding to the right and half a length behind my King!

This was a shocking thing for me to see. I immediately began to sob, because I believed the vision meant that I was about to die, to return on the Lord's Day with all the saints. The sobbing was because I did not feel that I had yet accomplished my mission here, and that perhaps, I had somehow failed and the Lord was taking me home. That sobbing was the end of the vision. For hours or days, I don't really remember how long, I remained in this state of believing my death was imminent.

Later, I was driving down the street in my van, praying about all this. As I was rounding a corner the Lord suddenly spoke to me saying; "YOU ARE RIDING WITH ME RIGHT NOW!" As I completed turning the corner I immediately understood these words I was hearing and my heart was filled with gladness. I let out a great shout of thanksgiving and praise to the Lord! I did not need to die to ride with the Lord! Right now, in my walk with the Lord on this earth I was riding with Him; hastening the fulfillment of Father God's eternal purpose! As God's sons take up the Lord's call and give their all to it they, too, are riding with Him—Hastening the Day of the Lord!

God Waits For You!

"God waited patiently in the days of Noah while the ark was being built." (1 Peter 3:20 NIV)

Here is more proof for the truth I'm declaring. God's servants, including Noah, must wait for God. We all expect to wait for God, and we must develop great patience to do so. But for those who walk with God it is a two-way street. We are "fellow workmen" with God, working on His great project together with Him. Therefore, as the instruments of His work, God also patiently waits for us, even as 1Peter 3:20 indicates. In fact, He does much more waiting than we do.

His patience sometimes seems like slowness to us, making us wait. Our waiting is actually caused from our own anxiety, not any laxity on God's part. In fact, Father God is always exactly on time. We however, often are not. We are often timid, self-willed, misdirected, and slow to listen and slow to obey. Our Father patiently waits for us to catch up with His purpose for our lives, all the while reaching out to help us grow. Since our free will is involved many of us never do choose to grow into all that God would have for us. On the other hand, some set their hearts and hands on the work God lays before them, refusing to be turned aside by any distraction—like Noah. Either way God waits on the response of His sons.

God Waits To Be Glorified In His People

In Noah's day God's patience waited for the ark to be built. That was a huge project that demanded total commitment from Noah and his family. In effect, they had to die to the world and all worldly aspirations, setting their hopes on a new world that had not yet come. But one they could see by faith. Everything in the world would have to take second place to God's work. Father YHWH was the Great Architect and Noah, assisted by his family, was the builder. Every morning when they got up that daunting project was there before them...day...after day... after day. Days turned into years and years into decades. During all that, life's everyday needs did not stop simply because they had work to do. Neither did the ridicule of the world. Yet, Noah walked with God and God is faithful. So even as God waited He faithfully strengthened Noah, and through Noah Noah's family, and guided them through.

Just as a gigantic building project was at the center of God's plan in Noah's day, so it is today. Only now the stuff of God's building project is not wood and caulking; but flesh, blood and spirit. God is still the Great Architect, the Son is the Builder and we are at once His fellow builders and the building. What is being raised up is a people molded individually and corporately after the image of God's Son to be His Glory in the earth—to function in The Spirit according to God's Eternal Order. This is so that the Glory of the Heavenly Father will be revealed on this earth in human flesh! This mystery is great. God's plan has always envisioned such a people glorifying Him in the midst of this world. Even now God is waiting patiently for His great plan to be brought into reality. The Great Day of God will not come until the fulfillment of God's plan to have such a people comes first—anymore than the Flood could come until the ark was built. So God waits. He waits for us to speed, to hasten, His Great Day.

The Spirit and the Word thus converge, both confirming the word for this hour: God's men must boldly rise up as instruments of God's Glory—to SPEED THE DAY OF THE COMING OF THE LORD!

FOOTNOTES:

[1] See *The Incredible Discovery Of Noah's Ark*, Sellier & Balsiger, 1995. For more scientific information on the Flood see *The Genesis Flood* by Professor H. M. Morris, *The Deluge Story in Stone*, by B. C. Nelson, 1949, *The Flood in the Light of the Bible, Geology, and Archaeology*, by A. M. Rehwinkle, 1957, and many others in the bibliographies of these books.

[2] One of the best remaining artifacts of the pre-Flood world is the Great Sphinx of Egypt. Geologists have proven that it greatly pre-dates other Egyptian structures and that it was eroded by water rather than sand! Water in the desert?! The Flood is the best explanation for this. For more information see *The Mystery of the Sphinx* Livionia, MI: The Sphinx Project, 1993. (this is the expanded version of the video that aired on NBC that was hosted by Charlton Heston, 95 minutes, $29.95, 800-508-0558)

[3] On what day did the Flood begin? May 14, 2345 B.C., exactly. Chronologist Gene Faulstich, founder of the Chronology History Research Institute explains how astronomy exactly pinpoints the timing of the Flood events: "Astronomical dating is an exact science in which we can, with the aid of computers, examine biblical events in light of astronomical occurrences. We can take the chronology data given by Noah in Genesis during the flood, and with computers, convert this data into a meaningful calendar. We also note that Noah was on the ark for one solar year of 365 days, observed the Sabbath day, and even more important, the Noah Flood events synchronize perfectly with the solstices and equinoxes, as well as with the days of the week. In 1659, Irish chronologist James Ussher, without the aid of computers, placed the Flood in 2348 B.C. However, with today's astronomical computer technology, we're able to accurately determine that the Flood occurred in 2345 B.C., and that the first Flood rains started to fall on May 14, 2345 B.C. We're able to confirm all the events surrounding the Flood due to a solar eclipse which occurred at sunrise on May 16, 2344 B.C. - when he observed a bow in the sky after they left the ark three days earlier." *The Incredible Discovery Of Noah's Ark*, Sellier & Balsiger, 1995 p. 111. Amazingly, other astronomical information discovered by scientists may give us a clue as to what actually caused the Flood. Scientists (writing in the May 15, 1970 edition of *Science Magazine*) have determined, based on astronomical data, that the axis of the earth shifted in - you guessed it, 2345 B.C. - the same date the Chronology History Institute has determined the Flood started! (Why not? Astronomy IS an exact science). This radical shift of the earth's axis, perhaps caused by the impact of a huge comet, asteroid or other heavenly body, apparently triggered the devastating global flood and accompanying climatic changes occurring with it. Let us not forget that God has fixed another day to come just as firmly in His great plan—it is called the Day of the Coming of the Son of Man.

10

GET BACK IN SYNC WITH HIM!

The great wooden chest, filled with its precious cargo, rocked and swayed over the face of the floodwaters that were "exceedingly violent on the earth." God's design of the ark was perfect and Noah had built it "according to all that YHWH had commanded him." Thus, the partnership of God and His man had produced a craft equal to its task so that "the ark floated on the face of the waters." Far below the ark everything on the face of the earth was washed away - making Noah's death to the old world complete. Yet, it was not Noah who perished. It was the world. Coming through those floodwaters was a baptism for Noah and his family. An entrance from the old to the new life. From that point forward all things would be made new for Noah. In this God pointed forward to the greater salvation than Noah's that would come. The apostle Peter writes: "For Christ died for sins once for all, the righteous for the unrighteous, to bring you to God. He was put to death in the body but made alive by the Spirit, through whom also he went and preached [God's judgment message] to the spirits in prison [the fallen angels] who disobeyed long ago when God waited patiently in the days of Noah while the ark was being built. In it only a few people, eight in all, were saved through water, and this water symbolizes baptism that now saves you also—not the removal of dirt from the body but the pledge of a good conscience toward God. It saves you by the resurrection of Jesus Christ, who has gone into heaven and is at God's right hand—with angels, authorities and powers in submission to him. Therefore, since Christ suffered in his body, arm yourselves also with the same attitude, because he who has suffered in his body is done with sin. As a result, he does not live the rest of his earthly life for evil human desires, but rather for the will of God." (1 Peter 3:18 - 4:2 NIV [brackets mine])

Messiah suffered and died, passing through the waters of death, if you will, resurrected and raised up to the right hand of the Father—where He holds authority far above "angels, authorities and powers." As Noah was saved through the waters we also are saved through baptism into Messiah. Not that we are actually saved by the waters of baptism themselves, anymore than it was the water that saved Noah. It was Noah's act of faith that saved him even as our faith in Messiah, first demonstrated through baptism into Messiah, enables our salvation.

The purpose of baptism is not some sort of magic "removal of dirt from the body"—as if that could really cleanse us. It is much more like Noah passing through the waters from the old life to the new. In going under the water we die to this world and in being raised up we are identified with the new life of the resurrected Messiah—being made one with Him in His victorious transcendent Life we are granted a good conscience toward God. In the new life we live in Him and He through us to the glory of the Father.

Like Noah before Him, Y'shua lived on earth for His Father's will. And like Noah, Y'shua suffered the scorn of this world. Unlike Noah, Y'shua "died for sins once for all, the righteous for the unrighteous, to bring you to God." Through baptism we come to God by identifying with the death of and new life in Messiah—that new life being the substance of our salvation. More than a mere concept, God imparts something real as the response to such faith—pouring out into our hearts the same Spirit by which He raised Y'shua from the dead. If then we have the life of Y'shua within us, should we not also expect to suffer, even as He did? Should we not have the same "attitude" as Y'shua, being willing to suffer the scorn of the world to accomplish God's will? It is only when we have chosen that same course as Y'shua, actually accepting suffering as the cost of doing God's will in our lives, that it can be said of us, "He who has suffered in his body is done with sin." He is done with sin in the sense that his selfish anti-life nature and fear of displeasing that anti-life nature in others is no longer what motivates his course of action. Pleasing Father YHWH, even in the face of ridicule and suffering, is now the great underlying motivation of his heart. "He does not live the rest of his earthly life for evil human desires, but rather for the will of God."

Share The Sufferings Of Messiah

Many modern priests and pastors want to fill up their churches, so they often preach a message of equivocation and compromise. They leave the impression that once you are 'saved' or enrolled you are free to go on as before, so long as you attend and support the church. Since Jesus suffered for you, you are told, you don't need to suffer. Instead, Jesus will help you fulfill your desires for wealth, fame and whatever. Unlike the apostolic message above, you are not called upon to suffer, to be done with sin, and to live "for the will of God."

I'm here to tell you otherwise. Salvation in Messiah is meant to be an entrance into a life of sharing in the sufferings of Messiah to accomplish the will of God on this earth! If you won't "arm yourself with that same attitude" then you are absolutely useless in so far as God's purposes are concerned. You are like the rich young ruler whom Y'shua loved—but sent away because he was not willing to give all he had. To be a true disciple you must die to yourself, accept your sharing in the sufferings of Messiah, and live for the will of God.

If Noah had believed in God, but had not expressed that belief through obedience, he could never have been of any use to God. As with Noah - obedient works of faith are the outward fruit and sign of genuine faith in the heart. Without such works of faith there is no real evidence that a person does possess saving faith in their heart despite their having prayed the "sinner's prayer"—or having performed some other religious ritual. It is a trap to think we have the 'salvation' base covered so that we can selfishly go on with our own pursuits. It must be real and it must be total to qualify as saving faith—such faith will ALWAYS produce works of faith that are clearly visible to others.

Superiority Of God's Eternal Order

Noah's faith was expressed through his obedience to God and God's Eternal Order. It was how he lived day in and day out. Noah obeyed God and Noah's family obeyed Noah, who was God's man. This simple order of things had been God's way from the beginning. Though men, women and angels had rejected this simple pattern Noah and his family had not. They held to God's Order and overcame the world that had not conformed to it. See the power in that? One great lesson of Noah for us is this: God's blessings and authority flow through His headship order into God's man, into his family and from there into God's work in the world. This is eternal. The world may change and has changed—but so long as men and women are on the earth God's Order never will change. This fact has been forever proven by the showdown between all the forces of darkness on one side and God's man and that man's family on the other. God's Eternal Order wins.

Compare that to how we do things now. Do you see why God's glory has largely departed from the organized Church today? Because the organized Church has departed from God's Eternal Order. If we would see the full authority of Messiah and the outpouring of blessings exhibited in His People we must start here. We must restore obedience to the order of things through which God has chosen to work from the founding of the world.

The Message For God's Men

This book is necessarily incomplete. The reason is that there is just so much more that needs to be said. All the specifics of how we make the transition to a restoration of God's Order as a people - and much more - will have to be addressed. The most this first book could do is lay a foundation to build on in future volumes. Yet this much is clear: If God's men will take this message to heart and walk with God as did Enoch and Noah, restoring God's headship order in their hearts and in their families, then a living channel of authority and blessing will be opened up in this earth through which God can work. Then it will be God's own will and not the religious traditions of men or the control of human culture that rules the Assembly of God. Only then can there be one unified people in the earth molded after the image of God's own Son, showing forth the glory of God on this earth in human flesh! To have such a people has been Father God's desire from the beginning—and it is still His desire.

God's Treasured Possession Not Just A Dream

Do not doubt that God can raise up such a people in the earth. Do not think like those prophetically quoted by the prophet Malachi: "But now we call the arrogant blessed. Certainly the evildoers prosper, and even those who challenge God escape." (Malachi 3:15 NIV)

I do not deny that this is the very condition that seems to prevail both in the world and in the organized church in these days. Yet, let us learn from God's past dealings. Is this not the very condition that also existed before the flood of Noah's day? Did not the rebel angels and wayward human race see things exactly the same way as quoted above? I can almost see Enoch telling them that God's judgment was hastening forward only to hear them mockingly answer; 'evildoers prosper...and those who challenge God escape...that's just how things are—and how they'll always be."

Yet even while that wayward world continued on as if calling YHWH a fool Father God was at work—at work preserving a remnant as His own—as a vessel of His glory. Therefore, we should not be surprised that Father God would prophesy a similar scenario to be played out in the final days when the prevailing attitude would be the same as before the Flood. Look what Malachi prophesied would be going on, even in the midst of the atmosphere quoted above: "Then those who feared YHWH talked with each other, and YHWH listened and heard. A scroll of remembrance was written in his presence concerning those who feared YHWH and honored his Name." (Malachi 3:16)

Even now Father God is listening and hearing! He is no fool. In the organized Church and out people are showing who they are by what they say and what they do. Father God is holding back judgment so that people can show who and what they are—just as He did before the Flood. And God is making a "list of remembrance" of those individuals whose hearts belong to Him, who "fear Him," that is, submit to His authority, and "honor His Name" by living out His ways.

Why is Father God compiling this faithful remnant list? He Himself gives us the answer: They will be mine," says YHWH the Almighty, "in the day when I make up my treasured possession. I will spare them, just as in compassion a man spares his son who serves him. And you will again see the distinction between the righteous and the wicked, between those who serve God and those who do not." (Malachi 3:17-18)

Yes, there is a difference between those who seem to serve God and those who REALLY do! That difference is in the heart. Two men can go to the same church, sit in the same pew, and pay the same tithe—and even say the same thing. Yet one is serving God while the other is not. The difference is often what you don't see— what happens when each of them is alone—what happens in their hearts—what only God sees. YHWH says that there will be a time when He will show up the difference—make a separation—between the wicked and the righteous. And remember, this prophecy is addressed to those perceiving themselves to be God's people—so the separation it envisions is among them! The purpose of the separation is that God might "make up (His) treasured possession." —Even a unified holy people—the glorious Prepared Bride foreseen by prophets and apostles—to show forth His glory in the earth!

Fire Is God's Instrument

There is only one thing that can show up the difference between those who serve God and those who only seem to. That instrument of separation is righteous fire. YHWH says;

"Surely the day is coming; it will burn like a furnace. All the arrogant and every evildoer will be stubble, and that day that is coming will set them on fire," says YHWH the Almighty. "Not a root or a branch will be left to them. But for you who revere my name, the sun of righteousness will rise with healing in its wings. And you will go out and leap like calves released from the stall." (Malachi 4:1,2)

"Surely, the day is coming" says YHWH! SURELY...surely means certainly. It is certain that the day of fire WILL COME! When it does come it will bring a separation among God's perceived people between those who truly serve God and those who only seem to. The one group, to be shown up as God's treasure...the other to be burned up as stubble. Yet, it is not in the day of fire that our future will be decided - it is well before that day ever comes. It is in the day that YHWH prepares His list! Now is the time to give our whole heart to God as His holy instruments. Now is the time to "fear YHWH" ... "honor His Name" and talk to each other about Him.

The Restoration That Is Needed Now

Now is the time to purify our minds of merely human teachings to learn God's true mind and ways. Now is the time to give our whole selves to Him and His rule in our lives. This is the restoration that is needed right now—the restoration of God's Order among His people—and it must start with you and I—God's men.

What my shackle dream was about - and what this book is about - is that there are two ways to live. One way is according to the mental framework and system of this world that the enemy has been building since the rebellion. The other way—God's way—is according to God's Eternal Order by the power of the Holy Spirit. We have seen that God's way is patriarchal, with emphasis on God's man as a priest and leader in his family, and the family working together, all for God's unique purpose for that family.

My question is: is this how God's people operate today? The answer, mostly, is 'NO'. The Church has inherited the Roman, worldly, form of government that gives priority to the goals of the larger corporate body and its leaders - subordinating God's work in families through family heads to the larger body. Thus the pastor/minister/priest is thought of as having the spiritual leadership role covered for the family while the man of the family generally concentrates on more mundane matters. This system has weakened families because it limits the spiritual leadership of family heads. Since this is so, many men simply abdicate the spiritual leadership role all together.

As in the case of Noah, God moves through His men and their families. Because the organized Church presently follows a more worldly form of government this often brings God's purpose for an individual family into conflict with the local Church body. The leaders tend to want to have control over the spiritual direction of the Church. If God speaks through a family head moving a family in a way that does not appear to fit into the goals of Church leadership then a conflict results. The family must either abandon God's specific direction for them or risk being alienated from the Church. This should not be. As with Noah's family, God's purpose for each individual family is more basic to God's plan then the larger goals of any corporate body. Any assembly of God's people needs to be structured so that God's headship order is not frustrated by an artificial form of internal government. The true remnant of Israel organized together must move in God's Headship Order to succeed.

I should ad that the artificial church order has proven to be a failure time and again. When real trouble breaks out it is never strong enough to carry the day. Nazi Germany is one good example. The organized church failed miserably in WWII Germany. As a group they stood by voiceless as Hitler murdered 6,000,000 Jews—and anybody else He didn't like. But God's work through families, like that made famous by the Ten Boom family of Cory Ten Boom, is the only reason Christian's don't have to feel completely ashamed of their record in Germany. That family is a sterling example of what God can do through a faithful patriarch and a godly family. Many were saved, physically and spiritually, through the faithfulness of that one Godly family.

Let Those With An Ear Hear

Let me conclude with this simple statement - and let those who have an ear hear: As it was in the days of Noah so also is it today; tension between the darkness and the light is building toward the breaking point. We are fast approaching a time of trouble that will make Nazi Germany look like a stroll through the park. God is calling to His people to get ready—and getting ready means restoring God's Eternal Order in their midst. God does not change and His order of blessing and authority has not changed. Even now, as the storm clouds gather overhead in unseen heavenly places, its time for God's men to get back in sync with Him.